FIVE ECONOMIC CHALLENGES

ROBERT L. HEILBRONER & LESTER C. THUROW

FIVE ECONOMIC CHALLENGES

PRENTICE-HALL, INC. Englewood Cliffs, New Jersey
07632

Charts on pages 39 and 114, and tables on pages 68 and 71,
from *The Economic Problem, 6th Ed.*, Robert L. Heilbroner
and Lester C. Thurow. Prentice-Hall, Inc., © 1981.
Reprinted by permission.

Prentice-Hall International, Inc., London
Prentice-Hall of Australia, Pty. Ltd., Sydney
Prentice-Hall of Canada, Ltd., Toronto
Prentice-Hall of India Private Ltd., New Delhi
Prentice-Hall of Japan, Inc., Tokyo
Prentice-Hall of Southeast Asia Pte. Ltd., Singapore
Whitehall Books Limited, Wellington, New Zealand

10 9 8 7 6 5 4 3 2 1

Library of Congress Cataloging in Publication Data

Heilbroner, Robert L.
Five economic challenges.
Includes index.
1. Economics. 2. United States–Economic conditions
–1971- . I. Thurow, Lester C. II. Title.
HB171.H48   330.973'092   81-465
ISBN 0-13-321091-X   AACR2

ISBN 0-13-321091-X

For Torben and Ethan, and Zeke and Jonah

CONTENTS

INTRODUCTION

Like great threatening clouds, five economic challenges—inflation, recession, big government, the falling dollar, the energy crisis—loom over our lives. Who has not worried about inflation? Who has not been made apprehensive about the consequences of recession? Isn't the problem of taxing and government spending a national obsession? Although we may not understand very clearly what it means, do we not feel in our bones that it is ominous when the dollar falls and gold skyrockets? And is it not gradually dawning on us that the energy crisis is not just a matter of higher gasoline prices, but of an impending change in our way of life?

So we know the five economic challenges from their impact on our lives. But the challenges loom up for another reason. We do not really comprehend them. The challenges wrack America not just because of the damage they inflict, but because of the confusion they bring. We do not understand where the great storm clouds come from or what gives them their enormous power.

As a result, the challenges demoralize us. We listen to experts—or to politicians who have been drilled in their parts by experts—talk about the causes of rising prices and falling output, of the intricacies of government spending and taxing, about the outlook for the dollar and for oil, but we do not understand what they are saying. Worse, we often have the feeling that they do not understand it either. Thus the challenges are not only assaults on our economic well-being, but on our psychological well-being. They undermine our self-confidence, our feeling that we have the necessary grasp to set things right, to distinguish good programs from bad ones.

This book is aimed above all at dispelling that feeling of

insecurity, even inferiority, in the face of the five central economic problems of our time. Our primary purpose is to explain these problems in terms that are crystal clear, not only to readers of the financial pages, but to those who never get past the sports or fashion pages.

Just as a good mechanic can teach a lot about how a car works without subjecting his listeners to a lecture on compression ratios, so a good teacher of economics should be able to explain a lot about how the economy works without subjecting his audience to long, technical explanations. But the engine of an economy is different from the engine of a car in one vital way: Its parts are people. A mechanic may be able to fix a badly working engine by disconnecting or reconnecting things or by discarding worn-out parts for new ones. But when you fix an economic engine, you are disconnecting or reconnecting *people*—to work, money, opportunity. When you throw old parts of the engine aside and put in new ones, you are consigning industries, regions, cities, to hardship or good fortune. Thus an economist can never fix an economy the way a mechanic can fix a car. No matter whether he assures you that the economy will run faster and farther and more smoothly after his repairs than before, there are always human costs as well as human benefits involved. Changes in the economic machinery never lift everyone evenly, like boats on an incoming tide. Usually economic remedies spread their effects unevenly, making the rich richer and the poor poorer, or vice versa; helping the Sun Belt grow faster than the Frost Belt or the other way around; boosting one interest and leaning against another.

And so the *real* challenge—the challenge below the economics of inflation and unemployment, government spending and taxing, international competition and the energy crunch—is political. It is to find resolutions to difficulties that will be acceptable to the people who *are* the economic machinery. As we will see, it is not the economics of the five challenges that is difficult. It is the politics.

Bringing home that political meaning of our current economic plight is the second major purpose of our book, every bit as important as explaining the "economic" part of the challenges. We want to show that political decisions are inextricably mixed into these problems, and that every economic "solution" to these challenges is political, insofar as it will favor one group or region or constituency more than another. Our message is that the economy is not a machine and that economists are not engineers. The parts of the economy, no matter what fancy names we give them, are always people. The repairs, for all the economic jargon in which they may be clothed, are always political. The decisions are never just technical, but moral.

We have strong political views about many of the economic challenges before us—views that will become clear as we get into things. But our objective is not to try to impose our own political judgments so much as to make our readers aware of theirs. Our belief is that people want to have their economic predicament explained to them, but do not want their political minds made up for them.

Finally, a word as to how this book came to be written. For many years we have worked together on a college textbook.* After we finished the most recent edition, we felt that it contained five "lessons" that ought to be beamed at a broader audience than students. The gist of these lessons, sharpened and pointed, is the basic text of our book. *Five Economic Challenges* represents the economics that we feel our country must know to master its economic destiny.

Robert L. Heilbroner
Lester C. Thurow

---

*Robert L. Heilbroner and Lester C. Thurow, *The Economic Problem*, 6th ed. (Englewood Cliffs, N.J.: Prentice-Hall, 1981).

FIVE
ECONOMIC
CHALLENGES

ONE

COPING WITH
INFLATION

Inflation is the curse of our times, the bane of our existence. But if we want to understand why prices rise and rise, and not merely rail against them, we had better start by backing away a little from our immediate experience to gain some historic perspective.

Inflation is a very old problem. If we look back over history, we find many inflationary periods. Diocletian tried in vain to curb a Roman inflation in the fourth century A.D. Between the years 1150 and 1325, the cost of living in Europe rose four-fold. Again, between 1520 and 1650, prices doubled and quadrupled, largely as the result of gold pouring into Europe from the newly opened mines of the New World. In the collapse following the Civil War, the South experienced a ferocious inflation. And during World War I, prices in the United States rose by one hundred percent.

But there is something different about the inflationary experiences of the past and our current inflation. The difference comes out very clearly if we compare American experience before and after 1950. Prior to 1950 inflationary periods were regularly associated with wars. The reasons were obvious enough. Wars greatly increase the volume of public expenditure, but governments do not curb private spending by an equal amount through taxation. Invariably, wars are financed largely by borrowing, and the total amount of spending—public and private—rises rapidly. Meanwhile, the amount of goods available to households is cut back to make room for war production. The result fits the classic description of inflation: Too much money chasing too few goods.

Second, U.S. inflations in the past have always been relatively short-lived. Prices actually *fell* during the long period from 1866 to 1900, and again from 1925 to 1933. The hundred-year trend, although generally tilted upward, is marked with long valleys as well as sharp peaks.

The record is quite different since 1950. Once again the outbreak of war in Korea and Vietnam brought price rises, albeit relatively small ones. But in a vital way, contemporary experience differs from that of the past. Peaks of inflationary rises have not been followed by long, gradual declines. Instead, inflation seems to have become a chronic element in the economic situation.

Moreover, the inflation has not only been chronic and persistent, but it has been accompanied by considerable levels of unemployment. In the period 1960–1965, for instance, the rate of inflation averaged 1.6 percent and the average level of unemployment 5.5 percent. In the years 1975–1979, inflation jumped to 7.5 percent, and unemployment also rose, to an average of 7.0 percent. By late 1980 inflation was 9 percent; unemployment 8 percent.

The presence, side by side, of inflation and unemployment has come as a puzzle for economists. Economists have always known that inflation was almost inevitable for a system that was bumping up against the limits of its productive capacity. But it was widely believed that inflation would go away if we retreated from those limits and accepted even a modest amount of recession and unemployment. Now we know that that is not the case. Recession and inflation can exist together in a condition that has become known as *stagflation*— stagnation plus inflation. The economic challenge is really to explain inflation *plus* recession—a task we will attempt in this chapter and the next.

THE ROOTS OF INFLATION

What has caused this new condition of chronic inflation accompanied by recession? There is no shortage of proffered explanations. Some economists lay the blame on money. They claim that the government, through the Federal Reserve System, has consistently been generating too much money—not, of course, because the government wants to create inflation, but because the monetary authorities have not been able to stand up to the clamor for more credit coming from the public in general and business in particular. Then as inflation gets going, the government tries to rein it in with various measures such as high interest rates. The result is the worst of both worlds. The reining-in makes the economy choke and gives us recession, but it is not severe enough to cut down the amount of credit sufficiently to stop inflation.

We'll look further into the money question. But meanwhile, there are a host of other candidates for chief villain. One that is frequently heard is that chronic inflation is the result of concentrated private economic power. Often the power is deemed to be held by labor, which keeps demanding wage hikes larger than the system can afford. This jacks up prices and also boosts costs of production: result—inflation plus a drag on output. Economists on the other side of the fence agree about the concentration of power, but place it in the hands of big business, where it is used to hold up prices even when business is slack, and to restrict output in monopolistic fashion.

Power certainly is involved in inflation, but whose power? For every economist pointing the finger at the private sector, there are two pointing at government. Sometimes the problem is government regulation, saddling the economy with excessive costs of regulation, antipollution activities, and the like. Sometimes the problem with government is deemed to be just plain excessive spending, although there is a debate whether the excess shows up in a swollen military budget or a swollen welfare budget. Very often the culprit is the federal deficit, a favorite target of political candidates. And not infrequently the trouble is located in some *other* government, in particular those that set the price of OPEC oil.

Even that does not exhaust the possibilities. There is much blame on sagging productivity as the cause for chronic inflation coupled with recession. Or there is an explanation that links America's difficulties with its role in the world economy. There is yet another account that lays the initial blame on the inflationary effects of the Vietnam War and the subsequent persistence of inflation on the peculiar institution known as indexing—the fact that we tie more and more payments, such as Social Security or wages, directly to the consumer price index, so that when the index goes up, we automatically get a higher Social Security check or a cost-of-living adjustment in our pay. And there is talk that inflation simply reflects our state of mind—a desire to have more than we can afford, an appetite that exceeds our capacity to satisfy it.

Which of these explanations is correct? All—or nearly all—of them have something to contribute to our understanding of inflation. What is lacking is a coherent framework to put them in, an overarching account that will enable us to think about the subject without feeling that we have to single out one crucial element, or keep a dozen in our heads at the same time.

To our minds, that coherent framework can only be put in place if we start from an elemental—but often insufficiently appreciated—fact. It is that capitalist economies are easily disturbed. Wars, changes in political regimes, resource changes, new technologies, shifts in demand—all disturb the equilibrium of their market networks as stones cast ripples in a pond.

All through the history of capitalism we find these disturbing events affecting the tenor and rhythm of economic life, but the disturbances work their effects differently in different historical epochs. In Dickens's time, it is likely that the most socially visible and important consequence of the dynamism and instability of capitalism was the rise of an industrial proletariat, the ragged factory workers and slum dwellers of mid-nineteenth century London and Manchester. Later, when the industrial nature of the economy was beginning to manifest itself, the tension within the system gave rise to the sudden crystallization of a new economic species—the giant corporation, appearing like a vast iceberg amid the floes of small-scale business life. Still later, beginning in the 1870s, the selfsame nervous instability of the capitalist process made itself most evident and worrisome in the tendency of the system to go into long cumulative contractions. In the six-year slump of the 1890s, for instance, between eleven and eighteen percent of the labor force in the United States was without work.

It may not seem important to begin by stressing this deep-seated and long-visible instability of the market system. But once we place it at stage center, we can see that a pressing question comes to the fore: *Why does instability in our times result in rising prices rather than in mass unemployment?* To take a specific instance, why did the shock of higher oil prices in 1973 touch off a new wave of inflation? A comparable shock a hundred years earlier—say a sudden fourfold increase in coal prices—would almost certainly have caused a massive depression. What has happened between that day and this to alter the way in which the market system responds to shocks?

It is not difficult to answer the question. Profound changes have occurred within the social and economic structure of capitalism throughout the world. Of these changes, the most significant for our purposes is the emergence of large and powerful public sectors. In all Western capitalisms these sectors pump out from thirty to fifty percent of all expenditures, providing a floor of economic stability that did not exist before.

This floor does not prevent the arrival of recessions. The market system continues to be vulnerable to shocks and changes as always before. The difference is that a market system with a core of public spending does not move from recession into depression. The downward effect on production or employment is limited by government floors provided by Social Security and unemployment insurance. Cumulative, bottomless depressions are changed to limited—although persisting—recessions.

In addition, the emplacement of the new public sector has greatly increased the political responsibility of governments for the overall performance of their economies. That is why central banks cannot carry out the restrictive monetary policies that might bring inflation to a halt. Central banks can and do pull on the string to tighten money. But no government—at least none that seeks reelection—can afford to carry out an economic program of such severity that it will threaten the social contract to which the government is the principal signatory. When the monetary string is pulled too tight, an immense wave of protest descends on Washington from outraged contractors, car dealers, small businessmen, unions, frustrated home buyers. These are a constituency that did not exist in the old days—that is, they are representatives of a public which today strongly feels, as it did not in the 1870s or 1890s or even the 1920s, that the government has a *responsibility* to prevent recessions from dragging on or deepening. It is very hard to resist this public pressure. Sooner or later the monetary authorities relent in their anti-inflationary zeal. The monetary string is loosened. We breathe again. And prices resume their upward trend.

Related to, but nonetheless distinct from, the rise of the public sector, we can see another vast change when we compare capitalism today and yesterday. It is the element of private power we mentioned earlier, the much greater degree of organization and control that marks the structure of business and labor both.

We have already noted that one of the most striking differences between modern inflations and those of the past is that in former days, inflationary peaks were followed by long deflationary periods when prices fell. Why did they fall? One reason is that the farm sector—*par excellence*, the sector of small business, where prices fall as easily as they rise—was proportionately much larger then. Another reason is that it was not unusual, in the nineteenth and early twentieth centuries, for large companies to announce across-the-board wage cuts when times were bad. In addition, prices declined as a result of technological advances and as the consequence of sporadic price wars that would break out among industrial competitors.

Most of that seems a part of the past beyond recall. Agriculture today accounts for only three percent of GNP, and will never get back to 1929's ten percent. Technology continues to lower industrial costs, but this has been offset by a "ratchet tendency" shown by wages and prices since World War II. A ratchet tendency means that prices and wages go up, but they rarely or never come down. This is due to the increasing presence of concentrated big industry, to stronger trade unions, and to a business climate in which wage cuts and price wars are no longer regarded as legitimate economic policies, especially when everyone expects government to prevent recessions from becoming too severe. These rigidities also add to our inflationary propensities.

There are still other changes that have made today's system more inflation-prone than the system of a hundred, or even fifty, years ago. We are a more service-oriented, less goods-oriented, economy, and productivity rises less rapidly in services than in goods. We are more affluent and much less willing to abide meekly by traditional pecking orders in society. These changes also tilt the system toward inflation.

But inflation proneness is one thing and the actual advent of inflation is another. Our inflationary experience had its origins in specific events that started the process off, just as the depressions of the 1890s or the Great Depression originated in particular happenings of those times. In our case, inflation probably received its first impetus from the boost to spending that resulted from the Vietnam War. A powerful stimulus to inflation in other countries resulted from the manner in which the United States used its strategic position during the 1960s to "export" inflation to other nations through its international economic policies. And by no means least has been the effect of oil shock, first in 1973 when the Organization of Petroleum Exporting Countries raised petroleum prices from three dollars to eleven dollars per barrel, and then again in 1979 when oil prices jumped from thirteen dollars to twenty-eight dollars in the wake of Iran's revolution.

Here we must again pause to reflect. We have suggested that a jump in coal prices in 1870, comparable to oil shock in our time, would probably have had a different effect: Many industries would have had to shut down; steel production would have been dealt a tremendous blow; in all likelihood a great depression would have begun.

Why did the cost-push of higher oil prices result in inflation and not in depression? We have already pointed to background reasons in the presence of a much larger government sector and in the more rigid wage-and-price structure of industry. Now we must pay heed to an equally important transmission mechanism that has made inflation contagious. This is the presence of those indexing arrangements that keep various kinds of payment even with the cost of living. A few years ago Congress indexed Social Security payments so that the checks sent to retired people automatically rise as the cost of living rises. The same kind of indexing arrangements now affect wages and salaries in much of the private sector, or protect industrial purchasers of many commodities. Most people who work expect to get cost-of-living increases whether or not they have worked harder or better.

Indexing changes the way the economy works in profound ways. Higher prices do not serve as a deterrent in an indexed economy as they would in a nonindexed one. Inflation would be self-limiting if prices rose and incomes stayed constant, but indexing means that incomes stay more or less even with prices, as we have already seen. While this may prevent much social hardship, it also tends to make inflation a self-perpetuating process.

Thus when oil shock came, the cost of living was pushed sharply upward and for a moment everyone felt the pinch. Personal savings dropped in 1974 as prices jumped. Then after a little time, cost-of-living allowances (COLAs) began to take effect, and soon incomes had been given a compensatory boost.

Along with the boost in incomes came yet another inflation-transmitting change: Our expectations changed. We began to expect a worsening, not an easing, of prices in the future. Unlike the old days, when the prevailing belief was that what goes up must come down, in an indexed economy we tend to believe that what goes up will continue to go up. Moreover, *because* it is indexed, we are given the additional dollars to put our expectations into practice.

Expectations are a major transmission mechanism for inflation because inflations, like depressions, have psychological as well as actual causes and self-perpetuating mechanisms. The trigger for depressions in the past has usually been a failure of private investment, whether because of credit shortages or overbuilding or threats of war and the like. Once a depression began, however, it continued largely because a psychological factor was lacking—confidence, it was called during the Great Depression. In the absence of confidence, the rate of business spending remained depressed.

Whether pushed by rising costs or pulled by rising demand, an inflationary boost has a psychological perpetuating mechanism similar to the lack of confidence that weighs on business spending during depressions. The mechanism is that of expectations. The experience of inflation leads individuals to expect more inflation, in part because of indexing. They build those expectations into wage demands, into pricing policies, into household spending behavior. Expectations thus feed on, and justify, themselves. Inflations are difficult to stop because inflationary expectations keep them going.

Thus we begin to see that many of the explanations given for inflation unquestionably play a role in the chronic inflationary experience of modern times. Government is indeed responsible for inflation, in a way. So is the massing of union power in strategic places or the increasing power of business to resist price competition. Indexing and public expectations and the hammer blows of rising oil prices and all the other villains can be seen to play a part. The difference is that these various explanations now take their place within an overall framework of understanding.

Inflation—our kind of chronic inflation, accompanied by recession—comes about because capitalism has changed in its basic structure. It is now government-supported capitalism, power-bloc capitalism, a capitalism of widespread and deep-seated high expectations. Those structural properties are not going to change. There will be no massive disengagement of government, which is now woven into the fabric of the system as inextricably as is big business or big labor. There will be no dismantling of big corporations or powerful union organizations in the industrial core. There will be no scaling down of public expectations, no return from the philosophy of entitlement to that of rugged individualism. So capitalism will continue to be what it is—inflation-susceptible. And as we shall see, the very efforts to restrain that susceptibility punish the economy by pushing it toward or into recession.

COMBATTING INFLATION

Can we stop inflation? Of course we can. The measures needed to bring inflation to a halt are not difficult to devise, speaking solely from an engineering point of view. The problem, as we have said, is that economists cannot be engineers. Their policies have political repercussions. The problem in stopping inflation is to devise measures that will be economically effective and politically acceptable. As we shall see, that is a very difficult problem indeed.

Balancing the Federal Budget

One of the most commonly heard quick-cure measures for inflation is that we should balance the federal budget, if necessary by a constitutional amendment. Would that stop inflation?

The answer depends very much on how we would balance the budget. In 1980, for example, if expenditures had been maintained at existing levels, and individual income taxes had been raised by about twenty percent, the federal deficit would have been eliminated. The effect of higher taxes would have served as a downward shock. Inflation might have moderated or even stopped. There is an economic answer. The political question is: *Who would have voted for the higher taxes?*

Alternatively, tax levels could have been maintained or even cut, and federal spending might have been slashed. But where would it have been slashed? About a quarter of all federal expenditures in 1980 went for defense. Few politicians wish to cut defense spending. Roughly half of all spending went for health and income security. There was perhaps room for trimming here, but Social Security and Medicare payments together accounted for over seventy-five percent of this outlay. Cutting these outlays would not have been politically popular. Another ten percent of spending went to pay interest on the federal debt: Legally that could not be cut.

That left about $120 billion—a fifth of all federal spending. Of that amount, $86 billion went to states and localities as grants-in-aid. If that item had been eliminated from the budget, the federal government would have shown a substantial surplus in 1980. But state and local governments would have gone deeply into deficit. Would that have been politically acceptable?

Thus when we consider trying to stop inflation by cutting back on federal expenditures, we must look into *total* public expenditures—federal, state, and local—not just federal spending. In 1979, total public spending was in surplus to the amount of $14 billion, or 0.6 percent of GNP. There was no deficit to eliminate. That warrants repeating: *There was no government deficit to eliminate.* In 1980 the total deficit of all governments was roughly 30 billion dollars. This was a little over one percent of GNP. Would such a feather tilt the inflation scales?

To review: We could use cuts in federal spending to give a sharp downward impetus to the economy. The difficulty is finding the areas in which to do it. As far as the federal budget is concerned, remember that its deficit may be offset by surpluses in state and local governments. A few years ago a delegation of state legislators, much concerned about the need for stopping inflation, came to present their views to Tip O'Neill, Speaker of the House. O'Neill listened sympathetically to their plea for reduced government spending and above all for an end to that damned inflation-producing federal deficit. He pointed out the difficulties in trimming federal spending in many areas, but remarked that there was the large flow of grants-in-aid to the states and municipalities, the elimination of which would simultaneously reduce the federal budget substantially and turn the federal deficit into a surplus. The delegation lost its missionary zeal. So do most people who study the realities of government spending, not its wicked image. Will the Reagan administration discover the same realities? Very likely it will.

Using Tight Money to Slow Inflation Down

Tight money is probably the most widely used anti-inflationary policy in capitalist economies today. Does it work? Partly. Tight money has succeeded in reducing the rate of economic growth because it is harder to finance investment spending, and *perhaps* this has mitigated the rate of inflation. In addition, tight money may hold down inflationary expectations—although some critics claim that very high interest rates, which result from tight money, serve to spur on inflationary expectations!

The problem with tight money is one that we have already noticed. Tight money works its cure only slowly, but its pain is sharp and immediate. This leads to on-again, off-again economic policies, often called stop-go. When prices begin to rise too fast, the Federal Reserve takes measures that make it difficult for banks to extend their loans to customers, or that raise the rate of interest banks must charge to make a profit. Governments may also trim their budgets. Wage and price guidelines are often announced.

For a time, these stop measures succeed. The inflation momentum slows down. But then pressures mount in the opposite direction. High interest rates cut into home building. A slowdown in investment causes unemployment to rise. Tight government budgets mean that programs with important constituencies have to be cut back; army bases are closed; social-assistance programs are abandoned. Business and labor chafe under guidelines. Hence pressures mount for a relaxation. The red light changes to green. The money supply goes up again; investment is encouraged; public spending resumes its former upward trend; guidelines are quietly abandoned. Before long the expected happens: Prices begin to move ahead too rapidly once more, and the pendulum starts its swing in the opposite direction.

The trouble with tight money, in other words, is that it takes too long, meanwhile exacting a social price that people are not willing to pay. In England, Margaret Thatcher is trying doggedly to keep money tight, despite increasing cries of woe from all sections of the country, including the business community. Perhaps she will manage to resist these pressures.

Meanwhile, Mrs. Thatcher's policies do not seem to have attained their end. Tight money has greatly worsened Britain's recession, but after *two years* the inflation rate is *higher* than when the policy was begun. It would be our guess that the political cost of any policy that does not produce its announced ends will sooner or later become too high for any government to pay. We will see what happens in England.

A Major Recession

No one doubts that we could stop inflation dead in its tracks by taking really serious measures, such as bringing money expansion to a halt. If we were to stop the growth in the money supply completely, inflation would come to an end, probably fairly rapidly.

The difficulty is that such a monetary straitjacket would impose very large economic costs. Here we have the examples of West Germany and Switzerland to go by. Both these countries have deliberately introduced the kind of major recession that is sometimes advocated. In early 1980, for example, industrial employment in West Germany was twelve percent lower than in 1973. In Switzerland it was sixteen percent lower. As a result, inflation rates in these countries were among the lowest in the world.

Why do we not follow their example? The reason is that the unemployment in Switzerland and West Germany was almost entirely imposed on their foreign workers, who were simply sent back to their native countries—mainly Italy and Yugoslavia, Turkey and Spain. Scaled up to an economy of our size, the Swiss alone rounded up ten million workers and sent them home. Which ten million American workers would we send where? In fact, equivalent cutbacks in the United States would create unemployment rates approaching thirty percent.

Such a policy would very likely stop inflation cold. But the economy would also come to a full stop. What social and political consequence would follow from such a return to conditions of the 1930s cannot be foreseen; few are willing to find out.

Voluntary Controls

Another approach is to impose voluntary controls on wages and prices, often in the form of guidelines that suggest limits for acceptable wage and price increases, especially for major industries.

The idea behind guidelines is clear and correct. If everyone would agree to curtail his or her increase in income to five percent, the inflation rate would promptly drop and *no one would be any worse off!* Unfortunately, unless everyone cooperates the scheme will not work, and the temptations to cheat are enormous. Think about the situation at a football game. It helps everyone to see the game if all remain seated, and no one sees better if all stand up. But if everyone does stay seated, the few individuals who stand get the best views; whereas if everyone stands, the few who agree to sit down get the worst views!

For exactly the same reasons, voluntary controls have not worked well. Therefore, a number of proposals have been devised to make adherence to a voluntary program profitable as well as patriotic. Among these are the TIP (tax incentive plan) proposals that call for tax breaks to companies that hold wage settlements to agreed-on guideline rates. The tax breaks are intended to provide incentives for employers to resist outsize wage increases at the bargaining table; and if all companies agree to hold the line, then no compliant labor union will be disadvantaged.

TIP plans might work. The difficulty they present is administrative, not economic. They call for a degree of supervision and intervention on the part of government that is certain to create bureaucracy and to generate friction. That difficulty may well be worth the price, however, if milder measures fail to arrest the inflationary trend.

Mandatory Controls

Last on the list are compulsory controls, such as permanent or standby ceilings on prices or on wage increases. Such controls would have to be backed by heavy taxes: The controls are just sandbags along the rising river; taxes provide the necessary sluiceway.

If war broke out, we would impose such controls and taxes instantly and probably with a fair measure of success. This is because during war a spirit of patriotism helps enforce public compliance. In addition, the overriding necessity of mounting an effective war effort removes all the usual hesitations about the limits of intervention. If controls result in insufficient investment, the government itself builds (or subsidizes) the necessary new plant and equipment. If wage controls reduce labor supplies, government can draft citizens or freeze them in their jobs.

In peacetime these advantages are not likely to be present. No warlike patriotic spirit exists; indeed, the prevailing attitude may well be to find ways of evading controls and taxes. And public opinion inhibits the government intervention that might be needed to overcome the problem to which controls would give rise. In addition, controls are onerous. Detailed norms must be written and enforced. In the Korean War we needed eighteen thousand price-and-wage inspectors to make the system work. Perhaps the computer can replace some of these inspectors, but not all of them. There is no such thing as wage-and-price control without a large bureaucracy.

Thus the objection to mandatory controls is twofold. They are certain to cause a great deal of public irritation. And they will pose an endless series of difficult questions in deciding how prices or incomes should be adjusted as our economy changes, grows, and faces new challenges. On the other hand, controls have one major benefit. More surely than any other measure, they will stop the inflationary spiral. If other measures fail, therefore, and if inflation accelerates and public concern mounts, we may yet be forced to resort to this last and most painful policy.

Is there a hope of stopping inflation without controls? The basic problem is that we cannot stop inflation unless we lower some individuals' money incomes. With energy prices going up and productivity falling, we will also have to lower some people's real incomes. That is simply a matter of definitions, not of economics. The political question is, Which individuals should they be? Can we devise a method of sharing the cutback? If we really share it alike, there would be minimal costs, and we would be rid of the frightening experience of an economy running out of control—or under full controls.

That is about all that an economist can venture to say. The best cure for inflation is persuading and educating people to adopt policies that will bring inflation to a painless halt by having each and every one of us agree to limit his or her income. Our place on the scale of income distribution would not change, but if we all called a halt to COLAs and indexing and wage settlements in excess of productivity, we would bring the escalator to a stop.

That painless cure requires a high order of political persuasion—plus a high order of public consensus. Failing the ability to gain that, we have no alternative to policies that will impose the cost of stopping inflation on one group or another. Now the trick is to impose them in a manner acceptable to the country at large. This is where teaching tends to go out and preaching comes in. One economist wants to stick the cost of stopping inflation on one group, another on another group. Each has his reasons, his appeals to history, his solemn warnings.

Which is right? That is often very hard to know, because so much depends on political preferences. One economist is all for farmers and all against unions, and he will therefore plead for a program that encourages a free market in wheat but not in wages. Another economist, who sides with labor and not with farmers, wants control over food prices but not over pay packets. And so it goes: economists favoring corporations, consumers; the poor, the rich; the big businessman, the little businessman.

Which economist is right? There is no right. Stopping inflation can be achieved in many ways. Each will impose costs on some and will accord benefits to others. The costs and benefits that look good to one advocate will not look good to another. Thus the solution to the problem of inflation is not to find a magic economic formula. It is to develop a political program for sharing pains that appeals to the country at large as fair and equitable, and that imposes enough restraints on enough critical elements of the population so that the rolling juggernaut will slow down and come to a stop.

THE COSTS OF INFLATION

It must be clear from what we have seen that there is no likelihood that inflation will be rapidly and effectively brought to a halt. The political task is too difficult. The country is not ready to impose a solution by ruthlessly penalizing some group—say small business and unorganized labor, or big business and organized labor, or to agree to a general limitation of incomes that would be costless, but doubtless very bureaucratic and "socialistic" looking.

So we will continue to have inflation with halfhearted remedies. It is important, therefore, that we have a clear picture of what its dangers and costs are. For there are certainly real dangers imposed by inflation and real costs in stagflation. But there are also imaginary consequences, and we had better clear our heads of those so that we can pay attention to the real problems.

One of the imaginary costs of inflation is that it has been eating away at our real standard of living, that despite our bigger dollar incomes we are really less well off. This is simply untrue. From 1969 to 1979, real per capita disposable income—income *after* inflation and taxes and population growth—was up by about twenty-eight percent. Thus the average American is better off, not worse off, than he or she was eight to ten years ago—and much better off than he or she was twenty years ago. Only starting in 1979 was there any decline at all, and then only a small one. This decline was the result of the fall in productivity that began in 1979 and the recession of 1980. It was not inflation that eroded our well-being.

Then why the widespread belief that our living standards are declining? Probably the answer is a phenomenon that economists call the money illusion. This is our tendency to measure our real well-being by the number of dollars we get—not by their purchasing power. Money illusion brings very sharp psychological costs in a period of inflation because our real incomes—our ability to buy goods and services—although rising, lag far behind our money incomes—our pay envelopes. Take the period 1969–1979 again, before the recession hit. Over those years our money incomes rose by over 134 percent. That is, the number of dollars in the average pay envelope in 1979 was easily double the number in 1969. But the increase in purchasing power of those 1979 dollars was only about 28 percent, much less than the increase in their number. Thus we had the illusion that our real incomes had doubled, whereas in fact they had only risen by about a quarter.

Imagine that someone agreed to give you a present of $134 tomorrow morning along with the morning papers. When you opened the envelope, there was only $28 in it. Actually, you are $28 better off than before; but you had expected to be $134 better off. Are you glad or mad? Do you feel lifted up or let down? It is the same in the economic world. If we had experienced a real gain of $100 over the past decade, we would all be very content. But that would have been far, far beyond the limits of our productive capabilities.

Another reason for our general feeling of a falling income standard is that inflation turns many personal problems into social problems. In a market system some individuals are always winners and others are losers, either absolutely or by comparison. When there is no inflation, people take these changing positions as part of the economic game, as part of life. In an inflationary period, however, everyone has a rising *money* income. Those who are losers are those whose incomes rises less rapidly than the rate of inflation. In a world without inflation, such persons would blame their economic plight on bad luck or on bad judgment or on any number of other factors. Except during a great depression, they would not blame their misfortune on the system.

During inflation, however, because losers are still receiving money increases—although perhaps not enough to stay abreast of the cost of living—they tend to blame inflation for a condition that may not be the consequence of inflation at all. College professors may blame inflation for their falling real incomes when the trouble actually lies in the current oversupply of Ph.D.'s. Factory workers blame inflation for their very real pinch when the problem is that the rise in female workers and in part-time employment has been cutting into the work week, and thereby lowering weekly wages, even though hourly rates go up.

The confused perceptions that arise during an inflationary period tend to blind us to a very important difference between recessions and inflations. In recessionary times, incomes fall. Unemployed individuals suffer real losses in purchasing power. Moreover, there is no social gain to be offset against their loss. The purchasing power given up by an unemployed family does not appear in anyone else's pocket.

Not so during inflation. Here, the decline in purchasing power of one unlucky individual or group of individuals is *always* offset by a rise in the purchasing power of some other person or group. *That is because every rise in prices always creates a rise in incomes.* Perhaps the gainer is a strategically placed group of workers whose higher wages are the other side of higher prices. Perhaps it is a group of businessmen for whom higher prices will mean higher profits. But higher prices always mean higher incomes for someone, if not at home, then abroad. Inflation may be killing us, as we continually assert, but someone is buying those shoes at Gucci and those Rolls-Royce Silver Shadows.

Thus inflation is a zero-sum game—a game of redistribution in which you win what I lose, or vice versa. Recessions, on the other hand, are not zero sum, but negative sum: Losses incurred by some individuals will not be transferred to others as income.

In analyzing the costs of inflation, therefore, we always have to look for winners and losers. From 1970 to 1980, our *real* GNP—that is, the value of our gross national product after allowing for price rises—grew by $324 billion in 1972 dollars.*

---

*We will be using the initials GNP (or gross national product) constantly in this book, and although we will try to provide synonyms where they will be helpful, we had better take a moment to get the definition straight. *Gross national product is the dollar value of all the final goods and services produced in the nation.* (We say *final* goods because we only count up the last item in any chain of production; we count the value of each loaf of bread, but not also of the wheat that went into the bread.)

There are four kinds of final goods or services that go into GNP: the value of all consumer goods and services, such as shoes or transportation; the value of all business investment, such as new factories or equipment; the value of all government output, from missiles through firemen's salaries; and the value of the goods and services we ship abroad, minus what we buy abroad.

GNP is thus the figure rung up on an imaginary giant cash register that keeps track of the production of these four kinds of output—consumer goods and services, investment goods, government output, and net exports. GNP is therefore also a measure of the total amount of spending (*expenditure* is the fancier word) on national output, because no good or service gets rung up on the cash register until it is bought, which means that someone or some institution has spent money for it.

Finally, we should also understand that GNP does not include a large flow of spending called transfers. These are expenditures such as Social Security, or interest on the government debt, or subsidies to farmers, or unemployment insurance, which have no connection with production. Transfer payments rearrange incomes and are very important, amounting to roughly ten percent of GNP. But they are not created by the act of production and are therefore not included in any GNP totals.

Someone had to be receiving that larger income. Who was it? Just the very rich? The oil companies? The municipal workers? The answer is, All of us. We can see this if we look at the distribution of income. If any one group had gained a major share of our growth in GNP, income distribution would have changed. But a look at the next table shows that it has not.

Shares of Income by Family,
1970 and 1978

	1970	1978
The poor (bottom 20 percent)	5.4	5.2
Working class (next 40 percent)	29.8	29.1
Middle class (next 35 percent)	49.2	50.0
Upper class (top 5 percent)	15.6	15.6

Of course there have been some social groups whose well-being has changed over the last years, but those changes have not always accorded with our expectations about inflation. It has always been held, for example, that the worst losers in any inflation would be pensioners on fixed incomes. But the single most important class of pensioners in the United States—the recipients of Social Security—have been winners, not losers. This is because their incomes are no longer fixed. Congress has periodically hiked up Social Security benefits *ahead* of living costs, and has now tied those benefits to the cost-of-living index. From 1970 to 1980, the average elderly family slightly improved its position relative to that of the average family in the nation as a whole!

Striking losers in the last ten years have been stockholders, most of whom are to be found in the upper class. Just as conventional wisdom led us to expect that all pensioners would suffer during an inflation, so it was commonly believed that stockholders would benefit from, or would at least stay abreast of, inflation. Because stocks represented shares of companies whose assets would be rising in value as a result of inflation, they were thought to be a hedge against inflation.

That is not how things have turned out. Over the last ten years prices have roughly doubled. The stock market has remained essentially unchanged. This means that the purchasing power of a portfolio made up of average stocks has had its value cut in half. That is about as bad as the fall experienced during the Great Depression. Why have stocks not been a hedge against inflation? There seem to be two reasons. First, interest rates are much higher than dividend rates, so that many investors prefer to put their wealth into short-term bonds rather than stocks. Second, investors are simply gloomy about the future, mainly because of inflation. Rightly or wrongly, many think that a share of IBM is a less solid store of value than a bar of gold.

It is *possible* that inflation has exerted its impact painfully on lower- and working-class families even though the distribution of income is roughly unchanged. This is because inflation has been particularly marked in four categories of goods: food, energy, shelter, and medical care. The price of these four necessities has been rising almost fifty percent faster than the price of non-necessities, and the proportion of household budgets going for necessities is markedly greater among the poor and working classes than among the middle and upper classes. The conclusion is by no means clear, however. The category "food", for example, includes eating out, which has gone up a lot, and eating in, which has risen less. Joseph Minarik, writing in *The Brookings Bulletin,* Spring 1980, thinks that necessities—suitably corrected for such wrinkles—may have gone up *less* than the cost of living as a whole. Economic statistics are often more slippery than they seem, and must be handled with care.

Thus there are certainly real impacts of inflation both on the poor and on the rich. Some individuals may suffer badly, even if the average individual does not. Our analysis shows, however, that we must be very careful in assessing this average impact. *There has not been an overall deterioration of well-being,* even though it *feels* that way. Certain groups have been more severely hit than others; some groups are actually worse off than they were in 1975. For most of us, however, two decades of inflation have brought real, although often unnoticed, improvements in real living standards.

THE REAL THREATS OF INFLATION

Does this mean that we have been worrying needlessly about inflation? That is certainly not our opinion. Even if Americans have judged the problem wrongly because of money illusion or the deceptive impact of inflation, there are ample reasons to place it at the top of the nation's agenda of problems. Specifically, there are four reasons to worry about inflation: The first three are threats and the fourth is an actual cost.

Inflation Holds Out the Threat of Running Away

One of the most disturbing aspects of inflation has been its tendency to accelerate. From 1950 to 1965, for example, the average rate of inflation in the United States was 2 percent per year. During the last half of the 1960s, that rate had picked up to 4 percent. In the first five years of the decade of the 1970s it almost reached 10 percent. After 1976 the rate first declined but then in 1979 rose to 9 percent. In early 1980 it zoomed further, and for a time threatened to reach 20 percent, although that very high figure reflected the peculiar makeup of the consumer price index more than the actual goods and services that most people bought.

This pattern of irregularly accelerating inflation can be discovered in most parts of the world. In the ten leading industrial nations the price level rose by about 2.5 percent a year during the 1950s; by not quite 3.5 percent a year in the 1960s; by over 9 percent in the 1970s.

Undoubtedly inflation holds the *threat* of running away—of quickening its pace until finally the value of money drops to zero and we have a complete social and economic collapse. Even though actual runaway inflations (or hyperinflations) have been very rare, and in all cases the consequence of previous military or social disasters, the spectre of such a possibility is profoundly unsettling. This is probably the main reason we perceive inflation to be a danger: not so much for what it is, but for what it might become.

Inflation Threatens the Value of Monetary Assets

Closely associated with the threat of a runaway economy is the threat of eroding assets. Inflation eats away at the value of monetary assets such as savings accounts, insurance policies, government bonds, and the like. Moreover, as we have seen, it has also badly eroded the value of stocks, although this may change if the stock market begins to take a brighter view of the future, under a conservative government.

The threat of inflation is that it could wipe out the money assets of the middle and upper classes, as runaway inflations in the past have done. In individual cases, very severe losses may have been suffered. To date, however, most families with monetary assets seem to have stayed even with inflation, using their higher money incomes to add to their savings accounts or insurance policies. For example, during the years 1970–1980, the value of savings accounts has risen from $194 to $670 billion, more than enough to allow for inflation. Insurance policies in force have risen from $1,400 to $3,300 billion. Nevertheless, the fear of losing their monetary assets is acutely experienced by families who hold them, and it is not a threat to be dismissed.

The value of some assets typically rises during inflations. Land is one of these; works of art; antiques—whatever is scarce and deemed to be of lasting value. Some of these investments work out very well, others do not: The land you buy may turn out to be in the wrong place; the picture may be by an artist whose reputation fails. Most significant of all the hedges against inflation is gold, the magical metal. Economists have always pointed out that the value of gold is only magical, and that it is not intrinsically a source of value and a true hedge against inflation. So far, economists have been wrong, and gold has soared during the inflationary era. How high can it go? The answer lies with your estimate as to how stubborn or persistent are people's beliefs; if the past is any guide, they are very stubborn and very persistent indeed.

Inflation Threatens Financial Instability

Inflation brings serious distortions into the nation's credit structure. One of the most troublesome consequences of inflation is the way it affects the relationship between businesses and banks. In inflationary times it is obviously advantageous to borrow money at normal interest rates because dollars will be cheaper and more plentiful when it comes time to repay the loan. Therefore businesses seek to borrow funds—but banks are loath to lend, for exactly the same reasons.

Two results follow. First, interest rates go ever higher to compensate banks for the falling value of the dollars they will receive. The prime rate charged by banks to their most creditworthy customers was less than four percent in 1960, almost eight percent in 1970, and then rose to over twenty percent at the end of 1980. This puts a serious crimp in many kinds of investment spending, such as construction.

Second, banks refuse to lend for more than short periods of time. The result is that business has to take on short-term loans at high interest rates. As short-term debt piles up, the system becomes vulnerable to any untoward event that will prevent the regular refinancing of debt. If a bank or a municipality encounters trouble, the whole financial community becomes endangered. Thus New York City's threatened bankruptcy in 1976 brought fears of a general credit collapse. The liquidity of the banking system—its ability to absorb a loss without resorting to panicky measures to raise cash—becomes a matter of general concern, rather than a matter taken for granted. Thus the threat of large-scale financial instability is another very good reason to worry about inflation.

Inflation Keeps Us From Trying to Reach Potential Growth

These are the threats, not to be despised. But the real cost is something else: inflation. It prevents us from trying to use all of our productive power for fear that we may tip an acceptable degree of inflation into an unacceptable or outright dangerous one. *Thus the real cost of inflation is the unemployment that it thrusts upon us*—not only the unemployment that stems from high interest rates and lessened investment, but the unemploy ment that governments deliberately tolerate or encourage in order to prevent inflation from getting worse, or in the hope of making it better.

Unlike the imagined cost of inflation—the feeling that our living standards are declining—there is nothing imaginary about the cost of unemployment. A person who is without work suffers a real fall in income and a great deal of damage to his or her sense of personal worth. The production that is foregone because of a recession is foregone forever. There is no way of ever enjoying the goods that we do not produce.

The costs of unemployment are important enough for us to devote our entire next chapter to them. But we should recognize that these costs, however large, do not seem as significant to the American people as the costs or threats of inflation, however exaggerated. The reason is easily under- stood. The costs of unemployment are borne by a small minority of the population—as we shall see, a minority without much political voice. But the effects of inflation are felt by everyone. Thus it is not surprising that all over the world, the need to hold back inflation has been regarded by governments as being of much greater urgency than the need to remedy unemployment. Governments and electorates alike are ready to accept more unemployment in exchange for less inflation; they are not ready to accept more inflation in exchange for less unemployment.

Thus the real challenge of inflation is, as always, political. Who will bear the brunt of the instability of our present economic order? So far we have imposed that burden largely on the backs of the weakest members of the society—those who are unwillingly drafted to be its inflation fighters. The political—the moral—issue is whether we can find a more equitable and effective means of sharing the burden.

TWO

OVERCOMING RECESSION

Ask American citizens what is their *second* most worrisome economic problem and you will likely get agreement that it is unemployment. Unlike inflation, however, unemployment has not been high on the public's list of complaints for ten years. This is because large-scale unemployment is a fairly recent problem, the consequence of the economic recession of 1973–1975 and the downturn starting in 1980.

Because unemployment and recession are so closely linked, we had better begin by asking, What is a recession? The answer is very simple. A recession is a drop in the gross national product that lasts for at least six months. The word *depression* is used to refer to a severe drop, but there is no generally accepted definition of when a recession becomes a depression.

Exactly what happens when GNP falls or lags? The pace of business activity slows down. There is less demand for consumer goods and services, less demand for plant and equipment and other business items. Some businesses fire people, other businesses hire fewer new workers. Because our labor force is steadily growing as our population swells, even a small decrease in the willingness to take on new workers spells a sharp rise in unemployment for certain groups, such as young people. When a recession really deepens, as in 1980, it is not just the young who cannot find work, but experienced workers find themselves thrown out of work.

BUSINESS CYCLES

But why should our GNP lag? One reason is that a capitalist economy typically experiences accelerations and decelerations in its pace of growth—changes that we call business cycles.

Generally when we speak of business cycles we refer to a wavelike movement that lasts, on the average, about seven to

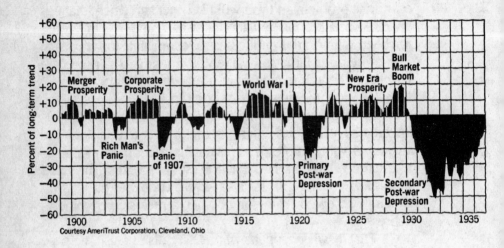

Courtesy AmeriTrust Corporation, Cleveland, Ohio

eleven years. In our chart below, this major oscillation of the American economy stands forth very clearly, for the chartist has eliminated the underlying tilt of growth, so that the profile of economic performance looks like a cross section at sea level rather than a cut through a long incline.

What lies behind this more or less regular alternation of good and bad times?

Economists no longer seek a single explanation of the phenomenon. Rather, they tend to see cycles as variations in the rate of growth that are inclined to be induced by the dynamics of growth itself.

Let us, for example, assume that some stimulus—such as an important industry-building invention—has begun to increase investment expenditures. We can easily see how such an initial impetus can generate a cumulative and self-feeding boom. The first burst of investment stimulates additional

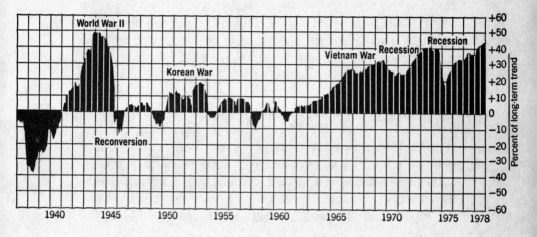

consumption, the additional consumption induces more investment, and this in turn reinvigorates consumption. Meanwhile, this process of mutual stimulation serves to lift business expectations and to encourage still further expansionary spending. Inventories are built up in anticipation of larger sales. Prices firm up, and the stock market rises. Optimism reigns. A boom is on.

What happens to end such a boom? There are many possible reasons why it may peter out or come to an abrupt halt. It may simply be that the new industry will get built and thereafter an important stimulus to investment will be lacking. Or even before it is completed, wages and prices may have begun to rise as full employment is neared, and the climate of expectations may become wary. ("What goes up must come down" is an adage that business still heeds.) Meanwhile, perhaps tight money will choke off spending plans or make new projects appear unprofitable.

It is impossible to know in advance what particular cause will retard spending—a credit shortage, a very tight labor market, a saturation of demand for a key industry's products (such as automobiles). But it is all too easy to see how a hesitation in spending can turn into a general contraction Perhaps warned by a falling stock market, perhaps by a slowdown in sales or an end to rising profits, business begins to cut back. Whatever the initial motivation, what follows thereafter is much like the preceding expansion, only in reverse. Downward revisions of expectations reduce rather than enhance the attractiveness of investment projects. As consumption decreases, unemployment begins to rise. Inventories are worked off. Bankruptcies become more common. We experience all the economic and social problems of a recession.

But just as there is a natural ceiling to a boom, so there is a more or less natural floor to recessions. The fall in inventories, for example, will eventually come to an end, for even in the severest recessions, merchants and manufacturers must have some goods on their shelves and so must eventually begin stocking up. The decline in expenditures will lead to easy money, and the slack in output will tend to a lower level of costs; both of these factors will encourage new investment projects. Meanwhile, the countercyclical effects of government fiscal policy will slowly make their impacts known. Sooner or later, in other words, expenditures will cease falling, and the economy will tend to bottom out.

We have spoken about business cycles as if they were initially triggered by a spontaneous rise in investment or by a natural cessation of investment. But more and more, as government has become a major source of spending, cycles have resulted from variations in the rate of government spending, not business spending. Cycles these days, more often than not, are made in Washington.

Take the six recessions (periods of decline in real GNP lasting at least six months) since World War II. Every one of them can be traced to changes in government budgetary policies. The first four recessions—in 1949, 1954, 1957–1958, and 1960–1961—resulted from changes in the military budget. In each case, the federal government curtailed its rate of military expenditure without taking compensatory action by increasing expenditure elsewhere or by cutting taxes. The result in each instance was a slackening in the rate of growth.

The 1969–1970, the 1974–1975, and the 1980 recessions are even more interesting. They represent cases in which the federal government deliberately created a recession through fiscal and monetary policies aimed at slowing down the economy. The purpose, as we know, was to dampen inflation. The result was to reverse the trend of growth. Thus it is no longer possible, as it once was, to discuss business cycles as if they were purely the outcome of the market process.

There is no doubt that the market mechanism has produced cycles in the past, and would continue to produce them if the government were miraculously removed from the economy. But given the size of the public sector these days, we need to look first to changes in government spending as the initiating source of a cycle.

LAGGING PRODUCTIVITY

So one cause for recession is simply the business cycle, whether made in Washington or Detroit or wherever. But there is a deeper cause as well—an undertow that pulls against the growth of GNP and that deepens recessions or makes recovery from them more difficult. This is a failure of the economy, after averaging out its cyclical ups and downs, to keep up to its path of *potential* growth. Potential growth is established by the number of individuals in our labor force and the productivity of those individuals. Normally both the numbers and their productivity—their actual capacity to produce wealth—grow each year. Taking boom years with bust, the number in the working force grows at about one percent a year. Taking the long record of the American economy as a whole, productivity per worker has grown at about three percent a year. Hence our potential growth is roughly four percent a year: the effect of a one percent growth in working persons plus a three percent growth in productivity per worker.

The problem is that for some time we have not kept up with that level of potential growth. Our next chart shows that between 1974 and 1979 the amount of lost output represented by this gap came to the staggering sum of $310 billion. In 1979 we could have added another $30 billion to GNP—$136 per person—if we had brought unemployment down from the actual level of 5.8 percent to 5.1 percent, the level now used to calculate potential GNP. In the recession year of 1980 the loss was far greater still.

Why have we fallen so far short of our potential growth? There are two reasons. The first is that we have deliberately pursued policies of tight money and fiscal restraint, hoping to hold down the rate of inflation.

But there is a second, more long-run reason for our disappointing performance. It is that our productivity has been dropping for some years. In the period 1973–1978, industrial productivity rose about 4 percent per year in West Germany, about 5 percent per year in Japan—but only 1 percent annually in the United States. This growth in productivity actually became negative during 1979, when output per man-hour in the nonfarm private business sector *fell* for a brief period at an annual rate of 2.3 percent. If that decrease continued, the Joint Economic Committee of Congress warned, Americans would suffer a drastic decline in real living standards. Indeed, our international position has already worsened because of the

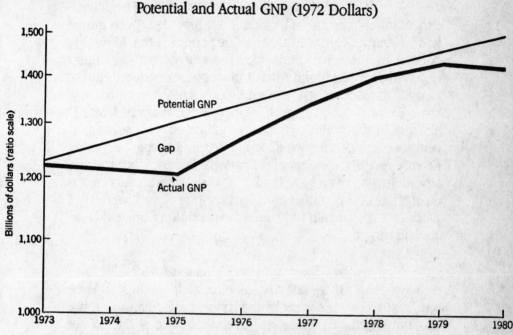

Potential and Actual GNP (1972 Dollars)

long relative fall in our productivity. We are no longer the nation with the world's highest standard of living, but the nation with the fifth highest standard, outranked by Switzerland, Denmark, West Germany, and Sweden, with Japan only 7 percent behind. Such international comparisons are always treacherous because tastes and styles differ so much among countries. But the basic fact that American living standards are now shared—or bettered—abroad is indisputable.

The long-term reasons why our productivity has fallen are fairly clear. We have been devoting a smaller fraction of our GNP to new plant and equipment than have our major economic competitors. Over the last decade, our investment has been roughly ten percent of GNP. West Germany's rate has been fifteen percent; Japan's, twenty percent. To make things worse, our labor force has been growing faster than theirs.

In addition, our R and D (research and development) expenditures have not only fallen, but may have been aimed less advantageously than those of our competitors. Mounting concern over the environment has dictated costly antipollution expenditures which add to cost but not to measured output. Finally, we have a much larger military establishment than any other Western nation. Over a quarter of our national R and D effort goes for military purposes, compared with seven percent for West Germany and four percent for Japan. A strong defense establishment may be a national necessity, but it exacts a price in slower growth. It takes a while before these causes exert their effects, but eventually they pull down our rate of production per man-hour. That is the condition from which we are suffering today.

The reasons for our recent precipitous decline into negative productivity rates is something else, however. Here one main cause is simply the poor performance of the economy itself. When the rate of utilization sags, we do not typically lay off managers, research departments, salesmen, maintenance staff, and the like, even though we may not be able to use their potential inputs fully. The result is a drop in productivity because there is a lot of unused manpower per unit of output. Conversely, when we move out of recession, productivity runs ahead of the economy because we can greatly increase production for a while without adding much to overhead.

Probably thirty percent of our most recent slowdown stems from this factor. Another twenty percent comes from a changing mix of our outputs. In the U.S. there are large differences in productivity among industries. In 1978 an hour of work produced not quite $6 worth of output in services (valued at 1972 prices), $8.70 in manufacturing, and $11.56 in agriculture. With so wide a range, shifts in our composition of output will have significant effects on our average productivity.

And after 1972, such a shift occurred. Output grew largely in the low productivity service sectors rather than in high productivity areas like electronics or agriculture.

Another thirty percent of our decline in growth can be traced to problems in specific industries—mining, construction, and utilities. Utilities have suffered because of high fuel prices which have led to sluggish growth and resulting sluggish productivity. Mining is an industry beset with health and safety problems which affect its working force and the environment. We are now moving more rapidly than in the past to remedy these problems, but falling productivity is one of the prices we must pay. Surprisingly, the biggest cause of our falling productivity in mining is the decline in our domestic oil production per hour of work. (We'll come back to that problem in a later chapter.) Construction has also been a very poor performer on the productivity scale. Perhaps this is only because its output is difficult to measure. Perhaps it is because we are building fewer large-scale projects where efficiency is high, and more small ones where it is lower. Perhaps it is because zoning and other laws make building more expensive. That accounts for eighty percent of our productivity decline. The source of the remaining twenty percent remains a mystery.

Obviously there is no quick fix to our productivity problem. But it is equally obvious that there are policies that would gradually, if not immediately, improve our long run potential growth. There is no doubt that measures to increase our rate of capital formation will sooner or later yield more output per man-hour. So will efforts to raise, or to direct more skillfully, our R and D expenditures. So will policies to assist "sunrise" industries such as computers to maintain their competitive place in the world, and to help "sunset" industries such as textiles to phase out their operations.

But such policies are easier to devise than to implement. Once again there is a political core to the economic challenge. Higher expenditures in industry may mean lower expenditures elsewhere—perhaps in urban renewal, perhaps in household consumption. Which do we want to do? Spurring investment will probably necessitate higher corporate profits, which many will oppose. Allowing unproductive industries to fade away will impose heavy burdens on their employees, who will fight with all their power to prevent their livelihoods from also fading away. Relaxing environmental protection standards will boost productivity—but at what social cost?

Thus even productivity—the least controversial explanation for our poor economic performance, and the one word in the economic lexicon that every politician salutes—has its hidden political elements. Raising productivity may hurt some people severely—for instance, workers or businessmen in big, inefficient industries that are deliberately phased out—while helping the public only in a diffuse sort of way. The programs that may be needed to boost our productivity will not, therefore, automatically gather unanimous support. On the contrary, some will be bitterly fought. Others will be lobbied for. All sorts of special interests will seek assistance from the government in the name of productivity, as all do during wartime in the name of national defense. Identifying the target of raising productivity is a safe and simple economic exercise. Carrying it out is a hard political struggle.

THE COST OF RECESSION

So there are two reasons for lagging GNP: business slumps and laggard productivity. Can we remedy them? Of course we can, just as we can remedy inflation if we are willing to take the necessary steps, or if we can find the right political mix of steps.

There is, however, a difference between inflation and recession, considered as economic challenges. The difference is that the cost of inflation, real or imagined, is spread more or less evenly across the population. In contrast, the cost of recession, especially its cost in unemployment, is sharply focused. As we shall see, that makes a very big difference.

For when we state that eight percent of the labor force is unemployed, this does not mean that every worker is laid off for eight percent of the year. It means that some workers are unemployed for long periods of time. Over fifty percent of the total number of weeks of unemployment is typically borne by individuals who are unemployed for more than half a year. Almost half of those who suffer long spells of unemployment end up not with a job, but by withdrawing from the labor force.

Let us think about this unemployment, for the moment, as the consequence of economic policies, such as tight money or reduced government programs, that we have undertaken to reduce the rate of inflation. When we examine the composition of the unemployed, we discover that our "inflation fighters" are capriciously drafted into national service. They come mainly from the age group sixteen to twenty-four, where unemployment rates are three times higher than those of adults. Women are thirty-eight percent more likely to be called up in the anti-inflation draft than men. Hispanics are seventy-five percent more likely to be called up than whites. These groups share two characteristics: They tend to be relatively unskilled, and they tend to lack political clout.

As we would expect, the group with the lowest unemployment rate is the group of prime-age white males. There are both economic and political reasons why they are the last to be fired in a recession. Yet, if we want our inflation fighters to come from groups whose wage rates are most significant in setting the national pattern, this is the very group from whom we should be recruiting our soldiers. Our point, of course, is not to urge higher unemployment rates for anyone. It is only to emphasize that unemployment, as an anti-inflation measure, is not equitable. Worse, as we have already seen, it may not be effective.

How serious is unemployment as a national economic problem? The record of the 1960s and 1970s is mixed. During the early 1960s, unemployment was at a level considered to be uncomfortably high—roughly between 5 and 6 percent of the labor force. This percentage dropped in the second half of the decade, partly as a consequence of higher spending on armaments.

It is the record of the 1970s that is disturbing. First we watched the number of unemployed soar to almost 9 percent in May 1975; a rate more serious than any recession in this century, barring only the 1933–1940 collapse.

By the end of the 1970s the unemployment rate was down to around 6 percent, and some economists argued that this was close to "full" employment for the nation. Their argument was based on the fact that unemployment among the prime-age white group had dropped to under 3.5 percent. By mid-1980, however, unemployment rates were once near 1975 levels.

There is no reason to hold that unemployment rates cannot be reduced well below that. But if we were to accept 6 percent as full employment, we would be accepting a much higher rate of unemployment than that for some groups in the population. We have already looked at the unequal odds facing our inflation fighters. Perhaps we should add that unemployment rates for black teenagers, corrected for those who have dropped out of the system—who are not at school, not at work, and not trying to get work—reveal unemployment rates of up to *90 percent* in central city slums! And even disregarding the pathology of the slum, black males bear twice the impact of unemployment that white males do, black females double the impact of white females, and all females 50 percent more impact than all males.

CAUSES AND CURES

What causes unemployment and what will cure it? The principal reason for joblessness, all economists agree, is too little

GNP—not enough spending (or aggregate demand, as it is sometimes called). When total spending declines, employers let workers go. *Thus the first cause of unemployment lies in too little demand, and the first cure lies in restoring demand to a full employment level.*

How do you increase demand? Basically, there are two ways. The first is to rely on the momentum, the drive for expansion, of the private sector. Since by definition that drive must be failing, or else we would not be in a recession, that means providing some extra incentive or stimulus for private business. These incentives can range from vague improvements in the atmosphere to specific and concrete assistance to individual businesses, such as the bail-out of Chrysler. On the list of stimuli we usually find such items as less regulation, less interference, lower taxes, easier money, and the like.

Undoubtedly measures of this sort can add steam to the economy. How much steam is another question. There is, for example, much talk about the crowding out of the private sector by the public sector in the financial markets, where it is said that the government mops up so much saving that there isn't enough left over for private enterprise. Statistical investigations have failed so far to show any crowding-out effect, so that we really do not know if business spending for investment would suddenly pick up sharply if the government withdrew from the money markets. So, too, with other stimuli, such as faster write-offs on plant and equipment, or less stringent antipollution devices, or simply less paperwork imposed by government. Probably there would be some stimulus, but no one knows how much.

The fact that we are uncertain as to how responsive the private sector may be to various stimuli does not argue against those stimuli. It only makes us cautious in our expectations. This caution is particularly relevant with respect to the probable effect of a *successful* program of stimulation on employment. For if the past is any guide, business may enjoy a very marked improvement in output or in productivity without a comparable increase in the number of jobs it offers. This is because much of the advance in industry may take place through investment which displaces labor, or through the growth of high-technology industries that use relatively little labor. All this is excellent for our growth in output and efficiency, but not for our growth in employment.

In the same way, if a program of business revitalization succeeds in tempting capital to leave old, stagnant industries and to migrate to new, more promising ones, that too will be good for GNP, but less good for payrolls. For in this case, the new jobs created in the Sun Belt and in the silicon sector will be offset by the lost jobs in the Frost Belt and in the lagging steel sector. What is good, even necessary, to overcome our sagging productivity does not in itself assure an end to the unemployment problem.

Last, we must recognize that the trickle-down of prosperity penetrates last and least into the crevices of the slums. The reason is evident enough; there are no businesses there to stimulate. No tax-incentive plan has yet been able to breathe life into the ghetto.

Thus a program to resuscitate employment must depend on public as well as private efforts. But public efforts can also be more or less effective in creating jobs, depending on their targets and channels. A program of public spending that concentrates on the public parks may not produce much national wealth, but it will produce jobs for the least employable. A program of high technology, such as space exploration, may create a lot of wealth, but relatively few jobs where they are needed most.

It makes a lot of difference, in other words, what sort of public measures we take against recession. But whatever their effect on employment, all government programs require additional spending.* And this leads to a familiar problem. As we

---

*Very likely, although not necessarily, more government spending also means incurring a public deficit—that is, borrowing the needed funds from the public rather than raising them through taxation. Deficit spending raises

rev up the economy through more spending, we soon reach a point at which prices begin to rise. Then we are back to deciding between inflation and unemployment as a choice of evils. Unemployment may be—indeed, we think unquestionably *is*—the greater evil. But the public at large does not seem to share this viewpoint. As we know, everyone feels affected by inflation, but only a few are hit by recession. Thus as the antirecession measures begin to show inflationary effects, the pressure mounts to call off the campaign, to let the economy "cool off," to draft inflation fighters to do their work.

Aggregate demand—or rather the lack of it—is the prime cause of unemployment. A subsidiary cause is automation, which may create unemployment or make difficult its cure even if the level of national spending is high.

Automation joblessness is a problem that vexes and worries us, partly because it is real, partly because we do not understand it very well. Technology can be a source of job creation, especially when it brings whole new industries into being. But machines can also displace people from established jobs—and may not create new industries to absorb them.

Looking back over the history of the United States, it seems as if machines steadily pushed people out of the agricultural sector, through the factory, and into the office. Fifty years ago it took almost forty percent of the work force to feed us; today it takes only three percent. The proportion of the labor force that works in manufacturing has been falling very slowly over the last fifty years. It is the service employments—mainly office, retail, and public jobs—that have burgeoned,

---

a hue and cry about the "burden" of the national debt that we create by this borrowing. It is always worth recalling that this "burdensome" debt is a prized *asset* for the millions of Americans who own government bonds. There is nothing more dangerous about government borrowing than about corporate borrowing. Both can be used to produce wealth. Both can also cause trouble when carried out in the wrong circumstances. The *economics* of the public and private sectors are much more alike than we realize. It is the politics that differ.

employing sixty-five percent of our labor force today compared with twenty-five percent in 1900.

Modern technology is more and more oriented to office work, the computer being the prime example. Will computer technology displace people from office jobs, or will it make new jobs? We do not yet know.

If automation in the private sector did bring unemployment, could we remedy it through increased public spending? We could, but perhaps not easily. For unemployment is not solely a matter of people losing jobs, but of people not being able to find new jobs. We can have unemployment that results from a lack of skills, or from a mismatch between existing skills and required skills, or because workers looking for jobs do not have the characteristics (such as literacy, or ethnic backgrounds, or education) that employers want.

This kind of unemployment is called *structural unemployment*. Because it is lodged so strongly in specific attributes of the individual, it resists the easy cure of higher aggregate demand. Business may be better for an employer, but he may find it cheaper to pay his existing work force overtime than take on and train a new labor force that does not meet his specifications.

The remedy for these kinds of unemployment is more difficult than for general lack-of-demand unemployment. New skills or new attributes (such as punctuality) are needed by the structurally unemployed, and these are expensive to impart. The Job Corps program of the 1960s, for example, found that it cost about ten to twelve thousand dollars to make an unemployed person—often a member of a ghetto group—acceptable to employers. Society was not willing to pay so large a fee, and employers also resisted (or asked large subsidies for) programs to hire and train "unemployables."

The high cost of retraining or of imparting desired work characteristics is one reason why structural unemployment is a difficult problem. Perhaps even more difficult is the question: For what jobs shall the unemployed be trained? Unless we very clearly know the shape of future demand, the risk is that a retraining program will prepare workers for jobs that may no longer exist when the workers are ready for them. And unless the *level* of future demand is high, even a foresighted program will not effectively solve the unemployment problem.

One solution to this problem would be to create a program aimed at making permanent jobs in specific areas of the public sector, such as the repair, maintenance, and beautification of our inner cities, or the care of the aged. Once again, however, we encounter public resistance. The government as the "employer of last resort" is a potentially powerful weapon for the alleviation of unemployment, but given the present temper of the nation, not one we are likely to use. If conservative convictions do not change, we may have to face the infectious danger of long-lasting structural employment as a result.

IS UNEMPLOYMENT NECESSARY?

There remains one last very important issue. Marxists have always argued that unemployment is not an accidental characteristic of capitalist economies, but a necessary and inherent element within them, essential for their successful operations.

As a case in point, Marxists point to the very large workless bottom layer of the American economy. First there are the officially acknowledged unemployed—over seven million in 1980. Then there are the underemployed, those who want full-time work but can get only part-time. These are another four million. Then there are one million who are not looking for work because they think they cannot find it. This gives us a very large "reserve army of the unemployed," to use Karl Marx's term for the jobless whose presence, he argued, served to keep down the wages of those who were employed. Really full employment, a Marxist would claim, would raise wages so high that profits—and capitalism—would disappear.

This is not an analysis to be lightly brushed aside. In Europe, for example, a "reserve army" has been created by importing cheap labor from Greece, Spain, Yugoslavia, and Turkey to man the great factories of the continent. When times are bad, many of these guest workers are forced to return to their countries of origin; so that the European nations, in fact, export some of their unemployed, as we saw in our last chapter.

It may well be, in other words, that some unemployment above the frictional level is needed to prevent wages from squeezing out profits or sending prices sky-high. Leaders in many countries speak candidly of the need to keep labor in line, and unemployment is openly acknowledged to be a disciplinary force toward that end. Some degree of unemployment may indeed be inseparable from the operation of a capitalist system.

But what degree? It is also clear that the levels of unemployment that have been generated and tolerated in the United States are not necessary. In Western Europe until very recently the levels of unemployment have for long periods been far below that of the United States, as the next table shows—a record of years in which European nations were not exporting unemployment but were enjoying a strong boom.

European nations have generally gone much further than we have in providing labor exchanges or in seeking to remedy structural unemployment, and they have been willing to accept a higher level of inflation as a lesser evil than a high level of unemployment. This superior performance has worsened considerably in the last few years, but Europe is still ahead of the United States in its anti-unemployment programs.

What is lacking in our nation, to date, is a willingness to place employment at the very head of all the benefits that we

Unemployment Rates
1960–1974

Country	Highest	Lowest	Average
United States	6.7%	3.5%	4.9%
Canada	7.1	3.9	5.4
Japan	1.7	1.1	1.3
France	3.0	1.6	2.3
West Germany	2.1	0.3	0.8
Italy	4.3	2.7	3.6
United Kingdom	5.3	1.2	3.2
Sweden	2.7	1.2	1.9

Source: *The Nordic Economic Outlook*, June 1975.

expect from an economy, a willingness to bend every effort to achieve the right to work for all. We may still not wholly eliminate unemployment, but then at least we could not be faulted for having failed to try. Need we repeat that this is a political question?

THREE

UNDERSTANDING GOVERNMENT SPENDING AND TAXING

Government dominates our economic life. Or does it? Many of those who most deplore the presence of government in economic affairs are also the first to tell you that government in fact is powerless to exert its puny efforts against the pressures of the market system. To many conservatives government can't *accomplish* anything. At best—or rather, at worst—it prevents the free enterprise system from accomplishing things. Government regulates industries that would serve the nation better if they were unregulated. It interferes with the system of rewards and incentives and thereby inhibits economic growth. It encourages the poor to remain poor. It spreads urban blight. It saddles us with debt. It is the worm in the apple, the root cause of every economic problem.

That is obviously not our own view of government. For better or worse, we see the public sector as the *only* mechanism by which a citizenry can intervene into the economic process when that process does not seem to work properly. *When problems arise from the market process itself* there is no—we repeat, no—way of coping with those problems other than by government. When the business system fails to distribute incomes to the old, the ill, the unemployed, what redress is there other than government? When industries dump waste into rivers or into the air, what means does the public possess to stop pollution other than the restraining hand of government? When corporations sell products that contain risks of which the buyer cannot possibly be aware, whether these are radial tires, birth control pills, or chemical additives in foods, what guardian of the public interest can there be save government?

That most emphatically does not mean that we look with favor on government meddling everywhere, on the proliferation of bureaucratic rules and regulations, on the inviolability of government secrets, on the police state, waste and extravagance, or centralized planning. There are as many ways to misuse government as there are to use it. *Our point, rather, is that government has become a central challenge because we have lost all perspective on it.* The issue, then, is not so much that government dominates our economic life—it is that government dominates our *thinking* about economic life. What government can and can't do are difficult questions to answer with certitude, but we cannot even begin to think about them as long as we perceive the role of government through lenses that distort its size and shape beyond all recognition.

Just as instances in point, people are always amazed when they discover that the states and localities are bigger contributors to GNP than the federal government; that the public sector in this country is one of the smallest in the Western world; that the per capita debt of the federal government, adjusted for inflation, hasn't changed for twenty years; that the proportion of the total labor force that works for the federal government is *three* percent (down by a quarter from the percentage of the mid-1950s); and that three quarters of all federal employment is in defense, veterans' affairs, and the postal service.

Nowhere is the confusion and misperception more pronounced than with respect to government spending and taxing. The enormous popularity of Proposition 13—the famous item on the 1978 California ballot that called for a drastic reduction in property taxes—symbolized not only a general revolt against government, but a profound and pervasive misunderstanding of government. Accordingly, that is the challenge to which we address ourselves here. Our purpose is *not* to plead for more taxes or spending. It is to try to get us to view this central economic matter in a different light—the light of facts, not fantasies; figures, not figments.

REVENUE

All governments need revenue. What is at stake is how much they need and how they get it. A good place to begin is to compare the level of taxation in the United States with that in other capitalist countries.

The table below gives us the answer. As we can see, the share of total GNP that comes to government as tax revenue is higher than ours in every country except Japan.

Percentage of GNP Raised in Taxes

United States	28.0
United Kingdom	32.8
West Germany	37.3
Sweden	43.5
France	36.9
Canada	33.9
Japan	22.6
Norway	45.9

In the light of these figures, we might wonder why Americans seem so incensed over the relatively low taxes they pay. This is a question that is closer to sociology than to economics, but it is important enough to warrant two speculative suggestions:

1. *Americans have always been disposed to regard government as an interloper, not as an integral part of a society.* It therefore follows that the threshold of discontent with government activity is lower in the United States than elsewhere. A story to the point is related by the sociologist Seymour Martin Lipset: Like the United States, Canada is a country with a frontier mentality. But look at the difference in the figures chosen by the two countries to symbolize this shared social experience. For the United States, it is the cowboy, symbol of individualism and disregard for government. For Canada, it is the scarlet-clad Mountie, the very personification of law and order.*

---

*S. M. Lipset, *The First New Nation* (New York: Basic Books, Inc., 1963), p. 251.

2. *Americans seem to feel that, relatively speaking, there is a lot of waste and extravagance in their government.* Wastefulness cannot easily be compared among countries, but casual observation leads one to believe that the perceived level of public efficiency and performance may be higher abroad than in the United States. Even conservative politicians in England and Sweden profess their admiration for the health and welfare systems there, although they wish to cut down on "frills." In the United States one often encounters the view that all public spending is a rip-off, and that waste is intolerably high. This may be related to the size and complexity of the United States compared with European nations, to the diversity of our population, and to the peculiar administrative problems of our federal-state-local governments. Or it may reflect a level of public honesty that is actually higher in "old-fashioned" Europe than in the United States.

What *should* the level of taxation be? There is really no objective way of determining that question. Nearly everyone would agree that it is possible to have too low a level of taxation, so that the country would be starved for public services; and it is certainly possible to have too high a level. Whether our existing level is a good one depends on our social objectives—a matter about which the public holds conflicting opinions.

There are two issues at stake here. The first is to determine the level of taxation best suited to moving our economy out of recession. This is anything but a simple determination. It hinges on whether we think that businesses and households would respond to a tax cut by spending all they saved in taxes, thereby creating employment and incomes; or whether businesses and households would *save* some of their tax cut, thereby making the level of employment and income lower than if government had kept the money and spent all of it. Liberals and conservatives disagree as to whether taxing-and-spending is essentially stimulative or depressive. No one really knows.

The second issue is more finely aimed. It asks whether the volume of government spending for specific tasks is high enough to achieve the desired ends of public policy. Do we spend enough on arms to give us national security? Do we spend enough on our national parks to preserve them for posterity; enough on research and development to underwrite a high level of productivity; enough on mail service to get letters delivered in time? Answers to these questions will vary from one area to the next. But they approach the problem of how much taxing we need from a different perspective than that of offsetting recession.

In this chapter we are not going to explore any further the question of how much taxing and spending we need. We have said all we can on that score. But Proposition 13 was not just a protest against the amount of taxes we paid. It was also a protest against the kind of taxes we paid, against the tax *system*. The challenge of taxing is therefore not only to decide how much revenue to raise, but how to raise it. The California voters who opted for Proposition 13 were specifically voicing their concern about property taxes; other tax critics feel that our income taxes are too high, or our corporate taxes, or our sales taxes.

Who Pays?

What is a fair tax? As with so many questions that affect public policy, there is no economic criterion for fair or unfair. But there are some objective measures that enable us to analyze the question more sharply than we do. Hence let us look at a wide range of taxes, from sales levies to income taxes, to discover what can be said about them.

We can start by recognizing that all taxes can be classified into three different kinds by their incidence—that is, by analyzing who pays them. Regressive taxes bear more heavily, in percentage terms, on low incomes than high ones; a highway toll, for example, is regressive because one dollar is a bigger part of a poor driver's income than of a rich driver's. Proportional taxes bear equally on all income groups. Any tax that takes a fixed percent of all incomes—say, twenty-five percent—would be a proportional tax. And a progressive tax is a tax that takes a larger bite—a larger percentage as well as a larger amount—as income rises.

There are no economic or even moral rules that enable us to say that one category of taxes is fairer than another. Yet most economists, politicians, and members of the public do not openly admire regressive taxes. Sometimes we favor regressive revenue measures, such as lotteries, which tend to bear more heavily on the poor than the rich, but then we find ways of rationalizing our decision, such as the popularity of such measures, or their convenience. On the whole, everyone favors proportional taxes or mildly progressive ones. But when progressivity goes too far—when very successful entrepreneurs are penalized by taxes that virtually wipe out all their incomes—we tend to call that unfair.

By these criteria, are our taxes fair or unfair? The answer depends, of course, on their incidence; and as we shall see, it is surprisingly difficult to determine what that incidence is.

To take the most simple-looking case, suppose that the state levies a five percent sales tax on all commodities sold at retail. Who pays such a tax? The question seems nonsensical. Doesn't the consumer pay the tax? Not all of it. When the state levies a sales tax, the cost of the taxed commodity rises. Because the cost of the commodity is higher, less of it is sold— gasoline or liquor or cigarette sales, for example, always suffer when taxes are placed on them. It follows that the sales tax must affect individuals other than just the buyers. The seller of the commodity must bear some of the tax because his sales have declined and presumably so has his income. The workers or other suppliers of services who produce the commodity will also be penalized, because less of the taxed commodity will be bought and therefore fewer people will be employed making it. In other words, the incidence, or burden, of a tax is often much more complex than appears on the surface.

Are sales taxes fair or unfair? Perhaps we can see how difficult it is to answer the question. Even in what seems to be a clearcut case, we have to know two things: First, we must know how much of the tax is shifted forward to the consumer, how much is absorbed by the seller or producer, and how much is shifted backward to workers or other suppliers. That requires a knowledge of demand and supply that we often do not possess.

Second, to determine how much of a sales tax is paid by any one person, we have to know the extent to which that individual is a consumer, a producer, or a supplier. Think about the impact of a twenty-five-cent tax per pack of cigarettes on a tobacconist who does not smoke but who owns ten shares of American Tobacco. Such are the difficulties of coming to clear-cut pronouncements about tax incidence.

Nonetheless, we can venture one generalization. A sales tax on necessities is bound to be much more regressive than one on luxuries. This is because necessities, such as food, bulk larger in the budgets of low-income families than of high-income families. On the average, food costs absorb about thirty percent of an eight-thousand dollar family budget, in contrast with just over twenty percent of an eighteen-thousand dollar budget. Therefore sales taxes on necessities are regressive. By way of contrast, sales taxes on luxuries may be progressive, if they are levied only on goods bought by upper-class families. A sales tax on yachts will have a very different incidence on rich and poor than a sales tax on gasoline or on retail items in general.

What about the incidence of a personal income tax? At one level, this is the simplest tax to discuss in terms of its incidence. If we are taxed on our net incomes, we have only one way of shifting the tax. This is to work less, thereby lowering our incomes. In theory, high income-tax rates might deter people from working. Income taxes lessen the utility of additional work because they take away some of the money income we derive from it. Therefore they may increase our preference for nonwork—leisure.

Actually, studies indicate that very few highly paid persons curtail their efforts significantly because of income taxes. Neither the number of hours we work nor the intensity of our work efforts seems to change if taxes increase or decrease. Economists therefore go on the assumption that income taxes are borne directly by the individuals who pay them, and that they do not significantly alter work habits.

Income taxes may, however, change income-tax payment habits. When taxes are felt to be high, people find means of avoiding them. In Sweden, for example, where marginal tax rates go above the eighty percent range, there is a widespread resort to nonmonetary forms of income, or to payments that escape the tax collector's gaze. A lawyer will offer advice free to a carpenter in exchange for a weekend's work on the lawyer's garage. A house painter, asked to submit an estimate, gives two figures: a very high one if the transaction will be reported to the government, and a much lower one if the job will be paid in cash.

Even in the United States, where marginal tax rates are far below Swedish levels, unreported income may be very large. Guesses on its size run into the tens of billions. And then there is the search for loopholes—legal ways of avoiding income. We will come to those shortly.

Income taxes levied by federal, state, or local (usually municipal) authorities are generally progressive in their structure. By and large, the rate of taxes rises as income rises: The federal income tax, for example, begins at fourteen percent and increases to fifty percent at a taxable income level of

$44,000 for a married couple. (It goes to seventy percent on property income.)

However, there is a great deal of difference between rates on paper and actual income taxes paid by families. This is because we do not pay taxes on our total or gross income, but on our taxable incomes. Taxable incomes are our gross incomes less various exemptions and deductions permitted by law. For example, we are allowed to deduct one thousand dollars for each dependent (including ourselves) in figuring our income tax. We can deduct interest that we pay, which is usually interest on mortgages on our houses. We can deduct all state and local taxes from our federal income tax. We can take off charitable contributions, legitimate business expenses, and a long list of other items.

Deductions affect the incidence of the income-tax structure in two ways. In the first place, they often create horizontal inequities. Two families or individuals with identical incomes may pay very different taxes because one can use a deduction and one cannot. For years, owners of oil properties enjoyed a deduction known as a depletion allowance. It enabled them to reduce their taxable income from oil by as much as a third below the actual oil income. Owners of state and local bonds have for years enjoyed the privilege of not paying any federal tax on the interest from these bonds. Thus two households, side by side in identical houses, enjoying identical incomes, may pay hugely different taxes. Because of deduction loopholes, some wealthy people escape taxation entirely. In 1969, there were 761 persons with incomes over $100,000 who legally owed no federal income taxes at all; 56 with incomes over $1 million also paid not a cent of tax.

In the second place, deductions greatly lessen the progressivity of taxes. Deductions have this antiprogressive effect because a deduction is worth much more to a high-income family than to a low-income one. Example: charitable donations. A rich family whose marginal tax bracket is fifty percent, gives away one hundred dollars. As a result, its pretax income is reduced by one hundred dollars, but its tax is reduced by fifty dollars. The net cost of the hundred dollar gift is therefore fifty dollars in reduced after-tax spendable income. A poorer family, whose marginal tax bracket is twenty-five percent, also gives away one hundred dollars, say to its church. It thereby saves a tax of twenty-five dollars. Its spendable after-tax income is reduced by seventy-five dollars. Not only is this loss of spendable income larger in *absolute* terms than for the richer family, but it is certainly larger as a percentage of its total income.

Let us next take a look at the corporate income tax, the source of very substantial sums for federal government.

Who pays a corporation's income tax? Few questions are less certain, even in the economics profession. Some economists think the corporate income tax is essentially a sales tax borne partly by consumers, partly by the business (in the form of reduced income), partly by the workers or other suppliers who suffer a loss in earnings. Others think it is a tax on capital, serving to reduce the flow of capital into the corporate sector. Still others believe that its impact cannot be clearly depicted because most corporate income taxes are paid by big oligopolistic companies who may use tax increases as an excuse to raise prices in their industry, laying the blame for this on the government. Some economists even go so far as to say that one of the virtues of the corporate tax is that no one can state with certainty who pays it; therefore it serves as an excellent way for the government to raise money without clearly imposing a tax on anyone!

Many critics claim that corporate taxes are unfair because they tax the owners of corporations twice on the income their companies have earned. They are taxed once when the corporation pays half of its income to the government—income that would otherwise belong to the share owner. And they are taxed again when dividends are paid and the owners receive their income.

This is a good illustration of misperception from the liberal side of the political spectrum. Many persons who favor progressive taxes would protest that abolition of the corporate income tax would aid the rich. Actually, if corporate income taxes were abolished and all corporate earnings were distributed to share owners, the bite on wealthy stockholders would be greater, not smaller, than today!

Social Security taxes pose another problem. There is no question who pays them. They reduce the income of the wage earner. Even the employer's part ultimately falls on the employee. The more interesting question is whether this tax is regressive.

At first glance there is no doubt in the matter. Social Security taxes today take 11.7 percent of all wages, half paid by a reduction in the salary check, the other half by the employer. This percentage is the same on all taxed wages, so that the tax seems quite proportional. But there is no tax levied above an established level ($29,700 in 1981), so that high wage earners pay a smaller proportion of their earnings than low wage earners. In addition, although Social Security taxes are taken from even the lowest earned income, property income of any kind—interest, rent, dividends or royalties—is exempt from Social Security. Thus, measured against total income, the Social Security levy is highly regressive.

Yet in the end, matters are not quite that simple. The pay-out formula for Social Security is set to give low income earners more dollars of benefit, per dollar paid in, than high earners. If we offset the regressive tax with the progressive payment schedule, the net impact of Social Security becomes slightly progressive.

The difficulty is that Social Security taxes are paid at one stage in an individual's life cycle, and the benefits are received at another, later stage. It is not easy to compare costs and benefits when they are separated by long periods of time. This problem is worsened because the ratio between the number of persons working (and paying tax) and those not working (and receiving benefits) is changing in favor of the retired population. An ever larger proportion of our population is living on Social Security, at much higher benefit levels than formerly; and these trends will certainly continue.

This means that it will soon become impossible to finance Social Security by the conventional Social Security taxes unless they are very greatly increased. Because workers are already grumbling at the cut that Social Security takes, it is likely that part of Social Security costs—perhaps the portion that finances Medicare—will be met from general tax revenues, and that Social Security ceilings will be lifted much higher. All these changes would further improve the overall progressivity of the Social Security system.

Finally, property taxes. Property taxes are very important sources of revenue for states and localities. They are also very hot political items since Proposition 13 put a ceiling on them in California.

One difficulty with property taxes is that inflation can raise the assessed value of real estate much more rapidly than it increases the income of homeowners. What happened in California was that owners found themselves unable to meet taxes that were mounting steadily higher. To be sure, homeowners could sell their houses at a profit. But to buy a new house cost just as much, and did not get around the problem of rising real-estate taxes.

Are property taxes always paid by homeowners? Not when they are levied on an owner who rents his property. Then the taxes are usually passed along as higher rents. Because rent payments are a more important budget item for low-income families than for high-income families, these tax-induced rent raises are regressive in their impact. For slum dwellers, who cannot afford to move, they may be terribly high.

Even in the case of a landlord, however, sometimes property taxes are progressive, not regressive. Suppose that property taxes are $250,000 per year on a building whose rentals yield $1,000,000 a year. Net earnings are therefore $750,000. As any investor knows, the building itself is worth a capital sum that will yield $750,000 at the going rate of return for similar properties. Suppose the market rate of return for such investments is 10 percent. At 10 percent, the capitalized value of the building will be worth $7,500,000. If property taxes are now raised, the capitalized value of the building will fall. Even though the taxes may be passed foward to renters, in the short run the heaviest cost will fall on the owner of the building, the value of which has been diminished.

So it is not altogether clear that property taxes are as regressive as they are thought to be. They are regressive only if we estimate their incidence on incomes. If we include their impact on wealth, they can be a progressive form of taxation!

Can we sum up the total incidence of the tax system? It must be clear that it is very difficult to do so. In the face of all the complexities we have mentioned, it is next to impossible to declare with certainty how much tax an average family in a given income bracket pays. Nevertheless, we can make intelligent estimates, and in the following table we see two such estimates, the work of Joseph Pechman and Joseph Okner, both of the Brookings Institution.

Notice the tremendous difference between Variant 1 and Variant 2. In Variant 1, millionaires pay 49 percent of their incomes in taxes. In Variant 2, they pay less than 30 percent. In Variant 1, a very poor family pays less than 20 percent of its income in taxes. In Variant 2, it pays 28 percent.

The difference between the variants lies in the assumptions that are made in each case. In Variant 1, where total taxation seems quite progressive, it is assumed that property

Two Estimates of Total Tax Incidence

| Adjusted family income ($000s) | VARIANT 1 | | | VARIANT 2 | | |
	Federal	State and local	Total	Federal	State and local	Total
$0-3	8.8%	9.8%	18.7%	14.1%	14.0%	28.1%
3-5	11.9	8.5	20.4	14.6	10.6	25.3
5-10	15.4	7.2	22.6	17.0	8.9	25.9
10-15	16.3	6.5	22.8	17.5	8.0	25.5
15-20	16.7	6.5	23.2	17.7	7.6	25.3
20-25	17.1	6.9	24.0	17.8	7.4	25.1
25-30	17.4	7.7	25.1	17.2	7.1	24.3
30-50	18.2	8.2	26.4	17.7	6.7	24.4
50-100	21.8	9.7	31.5	20.1	6.3	26.4
100-500	30.0	11.9	41.8	24.4	6.0	30.3
500-1,000	34.6	13.3	48.0	25.2	5.1	30.3
1,000 and over	35.5	13.8	49.3	24.8	4.2	29.0
Total	17.6	7.6	25.2	17.9	8.0	25.9

taxes are borne mainly by landlords and that corporate income taxes ultimately descend on shareholders. In Variant 2, which is roughly proportional and regressive at the lowest and uppermost ends, it is assumed that property taxes are passed forward to the renter, and that corporate income taxes lower consumers' incomes through higher prices, not stockholders' incomes through lower dividends.

Which of these variants is more likely to be true? *We do not know.* The actual incidence of taxation remains a matter for conjecture. We should note, however, that the uncertainties relate to the very lowest and highest incomes. Under both sets of assumptions, the tax burden for the groups that might be called the working class, the middle class, and the top five percent (although not the top two percent) are the same. Under both sets of assumptions, state and local taxes are regressive, and federal taxes are progressive—the two balancing each other out to produce an overall system that is roughly proportional.

Is this overall system fair? If by fairness we mean that our tax incidence should be mildly progressive, the answer is yes and no. Some elements of the system, such as Social Security, are not fair. Other elements, such as the federal income tax, are fair. Still others, such as the property tax, are sometimes fair and sometimes not.

To make things even more complicated, we must remember that the taxes a person pays depends very much on where he or she lives. There are some thirty-eight thousand taxing authorities in the United States, not counting the federal government. States, municipalities, water districts, school districts, transportion authorities, and a host of other agencies can impose public charges, fees, and taxes. The fairness of our personal tax situation is very much determined by our geographic situation.

It's very difficult, in other words, to pass any kind of overall judgment about the United States tax system(s). On one issue, however, everyone feels alike. *Whatever the values that incline us toward progressive or proportional taxation, few people would go on record as favoring preferential or discriminatory taxation. Yet that is, in fact, the kind of tax system that we have.*

Tax reform, in fact, is no longer basically focused on the question of progressivity or regressivity in general. The battle rages over the hundreds or thousands of loopholes that benefit small numbers of persons. Because the closing of any particular loophole would bring a tax saving of only a few dollars for most taxpayers, they cannot work up much enthusiasm in mounting an attack on any one provision. The beneficiaries of that provision, on the other hand, stand to gain enormously by it, and they mount an all-out campaign in its favor. Thus lobbying for individual tax breaks is intense. Lobbying against any one loophole is weak.

Here, of course, is where the politics of economics makes its entrance. What we have tried to show is how much

more complicated our tax system is than we usually think—
how difficult it is to know whether it is fair, no matter how you
define fairness. That is the *economic* side of the challenge of
understanding government as it is, not as we stereotype it.

The political side comes when we begin to consider
ways of making it fairer—that is, of changing it in ways that
accord closer to our moral preferences. Then the battle lines
get drawn as the interests of various groups are threatened by
proposed changes in the tax laws. The real test of a tax
reformer is to ask whether he or she is willing to pay a *larger*
tax if the proposed reform hits home. There are some
enlightened souls who genuinely place the public interest
above their own, but it is not surprising that most proposals for
tax change just happen to result in smaller taxes for the
proposer. This should lead us to two conclusions: (1) to
scrutinize very carefully the likely incidence of tax reforms on
those who urge them, and (2) to recognize that there is no
painless way of raising public funds. Someone must pay them.
The political core of the economics of taxing is, Who?

PUBLIC SPENDING

Taxing is, of course, only half the government's fiscal activity.
The other half is spending. It may help if we begin by looking
at the major purposes of federal, state, and local spending in a
recent year.

Now we want to ask a question that relates to our
present concern. *Is this spending wasteful?* As we ponder that
question, let us think how we would answer it if our public
output were produced by private companies for sale. Suppose
that our schooling, our road system, even our system of justice
were organized by private firms who sold education, transport
facilities, and justice to the public. Suppose, furthermore, that
these firms managed to cover expenses and make a profit.
Would any of their output be called wasteful?

Government Spending—1978
(Billions)

Purpose	Federal	State and Local	
National Defense	109	1	
Education	13	116	
Health and Hospitals	9	28	
Social Security and Welfare	157	42	
Police and Fire	1	23	
Transportation	16	24	
TOTAL	383	304	(includes items not shown separately)

The answer is no. The *only* criterion for waste in the private sector, so far as the kind or quantity of output is concerned, is the bottom line. The output of cigarettes, blue movies, shoddy boardwalk merchandise, or placebo medicines is not deemed a waste if the producing company makes money. Unsold merchandise is worthless, but the same merchandise, if tastes change, can be very valuable.

The public sector is intrinsically different from the private sector. With minor exceptions, it does not sell its output and therefore cannot justify it by pointing to market demand. Moreover, much public output consists of publicly shared things, such as defense or justice. For such public goods or services, there is no conceivable *market* test to determine whether the level of output is right. Instead we use a political test—voting—in place of the market. We'll come back to that in a moment.

Already we can see, however, that when we speak of public waste we have two problems. The first is to find a way of justifying the particular kinds of outputs, or the levels of outputs, we find in the public sector. How do we justify a defense program or a welfare program of a given size? How do we decide whether or not to spend money on a federal research project that some will call wasteful and others will call indispensable?

Second, to what extent can we use the criteria of business efficiency to analyze the operation of government agencies? How can we speak of the "bottom line," for instance, in the public sphere?

Let us start with the first question: How do we determine, in the absence of a market, whether a program should be undertaken in the first place?

The answer, as we know, is through voting. Where there is no economic mechanism applicable, we turn to the political mechanism. We vote for or against the general economic programs of candidates or parties. Within Congress or the state legislatures, our representatives vote again. The voting process is the subject of intense efforts to influence its outcome: lobbying, pressure from constituents, logrolling deals of many sorts. From this pulling and hauling emerges the national economic budget with its appropriations for different public purposes, a process duplicated again at state and local levels.

The process of voting leads to many difficulties in establishing an intelligent level of government spending. One of these difficulties is that, paradoxically, both increasing and reducing government expenditures are popular, vote-getting policies.

Most citizens will vote for government programs that increase *their* incomes. They will vote to lower those expenditures that increase the incomes of others. Thus if each of us were to scrutinize the government's budget, we could easily find areas to cut. The problem is, of course, that another citizen may gain from the very activity that we would eliminate. The objective then, is to find cuts in expenditures that will win voting majorities. As with tax reform, expenditure reform runs into difficulties because particular cuts in spending help most voters only marginally, while hurting some voters severely. Thus the beneficiaries of some expenditures form intense lobbying or pressure groups just as tax beneficiaries do.

For this reason there is an interesting difference between appeals for increasing government expenditures and for decreasing them. Expenditure increases are always discussed in terms of the specific programs to be expanded. This rallies a group of intense supporters and arouses only mild opposition from those who are not among the favored, because taxes will be only slightly raised. Conversely, when expenditure reductions are discussed, the emphasis is always placed on the general relief to all taxpayers, and the particular hurt to a few previously favored beneficiaries is passed over in silence.

The presence of staunch supporters and the absence of strong objectors demanding *specific* reductions tips the scale in favor of raising, not lowering, total expenditure. Obviously, this encourages waste in the sense of high expenditure. On the other hand, the bias in favor of raising expenditures does not mean that the public sector is therefore too large relative to the private sector. Many other biases exist in the system to reduce the valuation that we place on public spending and to inflate the value that we ascribe to private spending. Economic analysis alone can give us no ultimately correct division between public and private expenditure. It can only point to the political issues concealed within the economic argument.

Now what about the efficiency question? How does a legislator assess the worthwhileness of a proposed expenditure? Because a public expenditure is rarely planned to make money, a legislator must try to estimate the public benefits that will flow from the expenditure as an offset against its cost. These benefits may be fairly easy to calculate, as when a government agency plans to build a hospital and estimates what a comparable private hospital might earn. Even if the public hospital provides its services free, these services are surely worth that much to the public simply because it has been relieved of expenditures it would otherwise have made at a private facility.

But often the benefits of a project are exceedingly difficult to calculate. How can we estimate the benefits of a new road? By the tolls that might be collected? But what about the indirect benefits gained by townspeople who are now served more rapidly and efficiently? What about the businesses that spring up alongside the new road? What about improvements in the landscape if billboards are banned?

In point of fact, there is no accurate way of determining the bottom line of a public project. We can make more or less sophisticated guesses and estimates, but these estimates always contain a large element of uncertainty. We can easily overestimate—or underestimate—the benefit of a project.

Once a project is decided on for better or worse—a road, a school, a training program—considerations of cost effectiveness are exactly the same as they are in a factory, a private house, or any other private venture. The principle is the use of the most economic combination of inputs to achieve a given output. Here wastefulness has the same definition in the public and private sector. It is certainly not easy to translate the principles of efficiency, as an economist describes them, into the complex specifications of a construction job. But the aim is in no way different between the public and private sectors.

A second consideration that economists can offer to legislators is the concept of opportunity cost. The true cost of any public project (like that of any private one) is not the dollars it takes, but the alternative projects that cannot be undertaken because resources are committed to the first. The opportunity cost of arms is not measured in dollars, but in the alternative goods those dollars might have brought forth. And of course the idea works both ways. The opportunity cost of a high welfare program is, for example, the military might, or the road system, or the other possible things that the welfare expenditure might have brought into being.

Opportunity costs are difficult to apply to public projects because the returns from these projects, as we have emphasized, include so many nonmonetary gains. Hence, in practice, most legislators consider each year's appropriations in terms of marginal increases or decreases to existing commitments. Suppose, for example, that you are considering the federal budgetary appropriation for community development, a seven billion-dollar commitment in the previous year. In all likelihood, most of your discussion would be concentrated on whether the appropriation should be increased or diminished by, say, half a billion dollars. Your review of the opportunity costs of the project would focus on whether or not that half billion dollars would be a useful addition to the nation, compared with other uses to which those funds might be put (including their use by taxpayers if you decided to lower taxes by half a billion dollars).

Legislators rarely consider the opportunity costs of *entire* programs, which would require the dismantling of department structures with endless complications. So when we talk about "guns versus butter," we really mean weighing the benefits of one or two guns against one or two pats of butter. The programs themselves tend to become legitimated just because they're there.

Economists talk a lot about the regulating forces of supply and demand in the private sector. In the public sector the corresponding regulating force is inertia. Whatever exists tends to persist. This is, of course, one of the reasons why it is difficult to cut government back. That is not tantamount to saying, however, that government functions are therefore useless or wasteful or counterproductive. It is also difficult to eliminate private goods that are generally regarded as useless or wasteful or counterproductive, such as our ghastly TV commercials, when supply and demand keeps them there. The sword cuts two ways. There is waste in the market, defined by *nonmarket* criteria, and there is waste in the public sector, defined by *market* criteria.

This seems a good place to make a final assessment of the whole problem of how our resources are distributed by votes and by private spending. Many people look askance at every act of distribution by government. No one needs to be reminded of innumerable scandals having to do with influence peddling or abuse of the public trust by members of federal or state legislatures, which have resulted in the most blatant and outlandish squandering of wealth.

What we should remember, however, is that the voting process tends to be used, in a capitalist system, only when the market mechanism does not work well, or even work at all. The market is the principal method by which capitalism distributes goods—allocates them, the economist would say. It does so in a very simple manner. Each person who goes into a store, or who places an order by phone, or who enters the market in any other way, is entitled to buy as much as his or her income and wealth permit. This is also a voting system of a kind, only it is one dollar—one vote, not one person—one vote.

This way of allocating goods works marvelously well in many cases. It is quick, flexible, adaptable, stimulative. It solves problems overnight that tie up planned economies for weeks. It is a great saver of time and energy. Above all, it dispenses with the need for planning boards and rules and regulations and bureaucracy in general.

Just the same, *all* market systems have two failings. A few pages back we mentioned that markets cannot allocate some kinds of public goods. For example, there is no way of selling national defense just to those with the dollars to buy it. A defense system such as a navy will protect all citizens, whether they've paid for the navy or not. So, too, there is no way of excluding from the full use of an airways beacon those passengers on a plane who have paid tourist rather than first-class fares.

Because there is no way of selling public goods, we decide how much defense or air traffic control to provide by voting for them. If enough individuals want these things, we provide them. If not, not. The result may be wasteful, but it is a waste incurred because there is no conceivable method of consigning their allocation to voting by dollars.

Second, markets distribute certain kinds of goods in ways that outrage public sentiment. When a new vaccine comes onto the market, we do not want it to be bought up only by rich people. Or when a family falls into poverty, for whatever reason, we do not want it to starve on the streets. Therefore every market system excludes certain goods or services from the dollar voting system and entrusts them to the political voting system. We ration new vaccines by need, and we provide free or very inexpensive basic food or shelter to the destitute.

Therefore all market economies must have public sectors. It is impossible to have an economic system in which government would play no role whatever in the allocation of resources, where the dollar would decide everything and the voting rights of individuals would decide nothing. What is at stake is where to draw the line, not whether to draw the line. Here there is ample room for debate, but there is no room at all for contending that the political voting process is somehow an illegitimate intrusion on the marketplace. On the contrary, it is essential for its survival.

FOUR

DEFENDING THE DOLLAR

Americans have always been aware of a challenge from abroad. But that challenge has always been conceived in political or military terms. The idea of an *economic* challenge, at least during the last century, was never seriously entertained by the public or the government. America's place in the world economy was taken for granted—at the top.

That has changed, and changed dramatically, within a very few years. The former invulnerability of the American economy from foreign goings-on has come to an end. The American dollar, once the Rock of Gibraltar in a stormy world, has taken a terrible battering. Millions of American citizens are now directly affected by America's international economic position; all of us are indirectly affected by it. In a word, international economics has become a subject with which everyone should be familiar.

THE FALLING DOLLAR

The new situation has come home to most of us through headlines that have announced for some years that the dollar is falling. Sometimes the headlines tell us that gold is soaring, or that the yen or the mark or the Swiss franc have hit new highs. All these phrases mean the same thing—but what is that thing?

When the dollar falls in the international money markets, it does not mean that a dollar bill will buy fewer American goods. That is a very important point to bear in mind. Our dollars fall in *domestic* value as inflation raises prices, but it is entirely possible for inflation to cheapen the dollar at home— at least for a time—but not cause it to fall on the foreign money markets. Vice versa, it is possible for the dollar to fall abroad but to remain unchanged in its buying power at home.

When we speak of the dollar falling in foreign trade, it means only one thing: A dollar will buy less foreign money— German marks, French or Swiss francs, Swedish krona, or whatever. As a result, it becomes more expensive to buy *foreign* goods and services.

Suppose, for example, that you enjoy French wine. French wine is sold by its producers for francs, the currency in which French producers pay their bills and want their receipts. Let us suppose that they price their wine at twenty francs the bottle.

How much would twenty-franc wine cost in America? The answer depends on the rate at which we can exchange dollars for francs—that is, it depends on the price of francs. We discover this price by going to banks, the main dealers in foreign currencies of all kinds, and inquiring what the dollar-franc exchange rate is. Let us say we are told it is five francs to the dollar. To buy a bottle of French wine, then, (ignoring transportation, insurance, and other costs) will cost us four dollars (20 francs ÷ 5 = $4.00).

Now suppose that the dollar falls. This means that the dollar becomes cheaper on the market for foreign money. It follows, of course, that francs will become dearer in terms of dollars. Instead of getting five francs for a dollar, we now get only four. Meanwhile, the price of wine hasn't changed—it still costs twenty francs. But it now costs us five dollars, not four dollars, to purchase twenty francs. A falling dollar therefore raises the price of foreign goods in terms of American money.

Conversely, a rising exchange rate would cheapen them. Let us imagine that we were contemplating a trip to Germany. We inquire into the prices of German hotels, German meals, and the like, and we are told that we can do it comfortably for (let us say) two hundred marks per day. "How much is that in American money?" we ask. The answer depends, of course, on the exchange rate. Suppose the rate is three marks to the dollar. Then two hundred marks would be the equivalent of sixty-six dollars a day. But if the dollar happened to be rising, we could be in for a pleasant surprise. Perhaps by the time we were ready to leave, it would have risen to four marks to the dollar. It still costs two hundred marks a day to travel in Germany, but we can now buy two hundred marks for only fifty dollars.

We must remember, however, that international economics must always be viewed from both sides of the ocean. When the dollar rises, foreign goods or services become less expensive for us. But for a German, just the opposite is true. A German tourist coming to America might be told that he should allow one hundred dollars a day for expenses. "How much will that cost me in marks?" he asks his bank. The answer, again, hangs on the exchange rate. If it costs only three marks to buy a dollar, it will obviously be cheaper for the German tourist than if it costs four marks. Notice that this is exactly the opposite of the American tourist's position.

International economics has entered our consciousness because we have been reading about the falling dollar. We know now that this means the price of dollars, on the market for foreign currencies, must have been dropping. Therefore the price of other currencies must have been rising. It does not, however, mean that the price of *all* foreign currencies is higher than a few years ago. Our table shows the exchange rate of six foreign currencies against the dollar in 1975 and in late 1980.

Price of Foreign Currency in U.S.$

	1975	1980 (November)	% Change
German mark	$ .41	.52	+27
Japanese yen	.0034	.0047	+38
Swiss franc	.39	.58	+49
U.K. pound	2.22	2.40	+ 8
Canadian dollar	.98	.84	−14
Italian lira	.0015	.0011	−26

As the table shows, a German mark cost twenty-seven percent more over the period. But notice that an Italian lira cost twenty-six percent less! Why, then, do we say that the dollar has fallen, when it has actually risen against some currencies? The answer is that it fell against those currencies for which we had the greatest need. We do very little business in Paraguay, for example, so it matters little how many Paraguayan guaranis we get for a dollar. We do a great deal of business with Germany and Japan, both as buyers and sellers, and so it matters a great deal what happens to those currencies.

Why did the dollar fall? As with all price changes, the first task is to look at the supply-and-demand situation. And that requires us to investigate the nature of the market for dollars and other currencies.

Here we can best begin by mentally grouping into two basic markets all the kinds of dealings in which dollars and other currencies change hands. One is the market for currencies to carry on current, largely trade, transactions. The other is the market for currencies to carry on capital, largely investment, transactions. You will have no trouble following the story if you bear these two markets in mind.

The Market for Current Transactions

The first market in which currencies are bought and sold is that in which the current transactions between firms, individuals, or governments are carried out. Here the demand for dollars comes from such groups as foreigners who want to import U.S. goods and services, and who must acquire dollars to purchase them; or from foreign tourists who need dollars to travel in the U.S.; or from foreign governments who must buy dollars to maintain embassies or consulates in America; or from firms abroad (American or foreign) that want to send dividends or profits to the United States in dollars. All these kinds of transactions require that holders of marks or francs or yen buy U.S. dollars on the foreign market.

And, of course, there are similar groups of Americans who supply dollars to the foreign exchange market for exactly the opposite reasons. Here we find American importers who want to bring in Japanese cameras and must offer dollars in order to acquire the yen to make their purchases; American or foreign firms that are sending dividends or profits earned in the U.S. to a foreign branch or headquarters; Americans or foreign residents who sell dollars in order to buy lire or drachmas or krona to send money to friends or relatives abroad; or the American government, which uses dollars to buy foreign currencies to pay diplomatic living expenses or to make military expenditures abroad.

Taken all together, these supplies and demands for dollars establish what we call our balance on current account. As the next chart shows, this balance took a substantial fall in the early 1970s, followed by a sharp rise and then another fall. Up to 1968, foreigners were buying more dollars for all the various purposes of current transactions than Americans were selling dollars for those purposes; whereas since the 1970s, as the graph shows, the balance has largely gone the other way. What was the reason for this sharp adverse change in our current balance of payments? The next chart shows that it was mainly the result of a dramatic fall in our merchandise balance of trade. This is a submarket within the larger flow of all current transactions in which we pay heed only to those dollars supplied and demanded to finance imports and exports of merchandise.

Until 1971 the United States had a small positive balance on merchandise account. This meant that we were selling more goods and services abroad, measured in dollars, than the dollar value of the goods and services we were buying there. What has happened thereafter to turn the balance from black to red? The answer in part is the OPEC oil crisis, which

Balance on Current Account 1971–1980

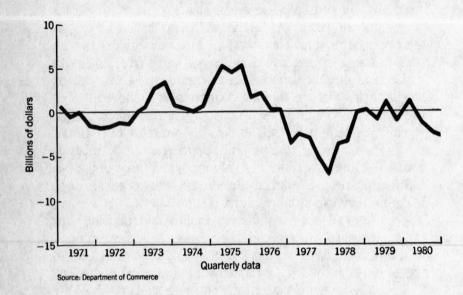

Source: Department of Commerce

resulted in a sharp rise in the number of dollars we had to supply to buy oil abroad. In 1972 our oil bill was five billion dollars. In 1974 it was twenty-seven billion dollars. By 1980 it had grown to 90 billion dollars.

But oil shock was not the only reason for the falling merchandise balance. The United States has experienced a long, gradual decline in its competitive position vis-à-vis the other industrial nations of the West, a decline attributable in considerable part to laggard American productivity. In addition, a number of other developments have tilted the merchandise balance away from America—the international agricultural situation, the respective inflation rates of the U.S. and its main competitors, and still other factors.

This is one major reason why the supply of dollars, needed for imports, came to exceed the demand for dollars,

Merchandise Trade Balance

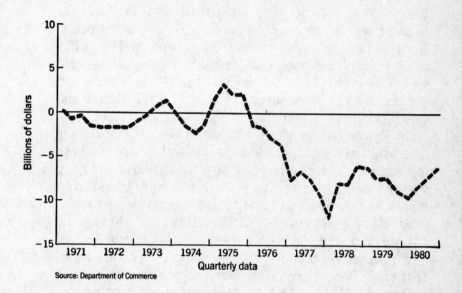

Source: Department of Commerce

needed by foreigners to purchase American exports. When the quantity of any commodity supplied exceeds the quantity demanded, its price drops. The dollar was no exception. It fell.

The Market for Capital

But the market for current transactions is not the only arena in which the supply and demand for dollars establish a price for dollars against other currencies. A second, quite separate, market arises to accommodate the need for dollars and other currencies to finance capital transactions, not current ones Here are such items as building or buying plant and equip ment in another country, or buying the bonds or stocks issued within another nation.

The first of these capital flows is called direct invest ment. It arises from the efforts of American firms (mainly

multinationals) to expand their ownership of plant and equipment abroad, and from the corresponding efforts of foreign
companies to do the same thing here. In 1978 U.S. firms
invested over seventeen billion dollars in foreign production
facilities, ranging from oil refineries to supermarkets, while
foreign companies bought or built direct investments worth
six billion dollars here. Subsequently in 1979 the supply and
demand for direct-investment funds also pushed down the
price of dollars.

The second part of the capital market is made up of
American or foreign individuals or firms who want to add to
their overseas portfolio investments of stocks and bonds. Here
we have Americans who buy stock in a Swedish firm or who
buy German government bonds, and foreign investors who
buy General Motors stock or U.S. Treasury bonds. In 1979 the
balance on portfolio account was also against the United States.
Adding direct and portfolio investment together, we had a total
of thirty billion more dollars being supplied in the foreign
exchange market in 1979 than were demanded in that market.
This too increased the supply of dollars and contributed to its
drop in price.

Why have we had such large capital outflows? Part of the
answer is that American multinational corporations have
grown faster than their counterparts here. We have heard much
in recent years about an invasion of Arab money into American
markets, but it has clearly not been nearly as large as the
continuing invasion of American money abroad. Between 1970
and 1978, U.S. direct investment abroad climbed from $76
billion to $168 billion, while all foreign direct investment here
only rose from $13 to $40 billion.

The negative flow on portfolio account arose from two
main stimuli. Holders of large liquid balances, such as the
treasurers of multinationals or wealthy private investors, park
their money where the expected rise in value is greatest. In the
seventies short-term money sought out European currencies

just like investors seek out the most promising stocks—and the dollar weakened as a consequence. Second, many private investors did indeed invest in the stock markets of different countries. The U.S. stock market has made an indifferent showing over the last decade compared with some of Europe's or Japan's stock exchanges. This too has led to a larger supply of dollars than demand for them.

Two more important influences bear on the capital markets for foreign exchange. One of these is the actions of central banks, who get into the act of buying and selling exchange to defend their currencies. We'll discuss that shortly. The other influence affects the nongovernment part of the market. It is speculation based on the price of foreign exchange that investors expect to receive in the future. If you think that the German mark will rise against the dollar, you can make money by buying German currency before it goes up. Thus there is a constant flow of "hot" money from country to country as private investors or multinationals move their funds around, hoping to buy cheap and sell dear. Until very recently, a great deal of this speculative ebb and flow has also gone against the United States, because investors have felt that the United States was irresolute in the defense of the dollar, and that therefore the dollar would weaken. Of course, by selling dollars and buying marks or yen or whatever, speculators have helped that very expectation to come true.

PROBLEMS OF A FALLING DOLLAR

We have just mentioned the defense of the falling dollar, and we must soon turn our full attention to that subject. But before we consider means, we had better think about ends. What are we defending the dollar against? What difference does it make to Americans whether one dollar is worth two marks or three? What difference does it make if the dollar—whatever its exchange rate—is declining to a lower rate?

Let us consider the first part of the question. Does it matter how many yen, francs, or pounds a dollar exchanges for?

Like so many economic questions, this has a political answer, for the exchange value of a currency affects different individuals or groups or regions in different ways. Suppose that the dollar is cheap. Obviously this is good for anyone who wants to buy a U.S. good or service, using foreign money. It makes travel in the U.S. inexpensive for foreigners. It makes American exports attractive. It makes American stocks or physical plant tempting to foreign investors. All this redounds to the benefit of U.S. exporters or hotel keepers or stock-brokers or owners who want to sell to foreigners.

On the other hand, a cheap dollar penalizes other groups. An American traveling abroad finds prices terribly high. An American importer finds that foreign wines, cameras, cars, sweaters are expensive—and so do his customers. American firms thinking of investing abroad are deterred by the high price of foreign exchange. All this is bad for American tourists, consumers, and multinationals.

Is there any reason for giving preference to those groups who benefit from the cheap dollar over other groups who benefit from expensive dollars? From the point of view of our national well-being, there is no particular reason to favor one over another. Is it better for a million consumers to buy cameras cheap, or for one hundred thousand steelworkers to have higher incomes? There is no cut-and-dried answer, only a contest of wills.

How, then, does a nation determine the right rate for its exchange, when cheap rates help some groups and expensive rates help others? The answer is that a nation tries to discover the rate that will roughly balance out all the supplies and all the demands for its currency, so that it has a stable, "equilibrium" relationship between its own currency and those of other nations.

What happens if a country does not have such an equilibrium relationship? If the rate is too high, there will be a stimulus for the country to buy imports and a deterrent to its exports. The result will be unemployment in its export industries and, as a consequence, unemployment elsewhere. Perhaps the most famous case of an overvalued currency was that of England following World War I, when Winston Churchill, then Chancellor of the Exchequer, tried to establish an exchange rate of £1 = $5. At that rate the demand for pounds was far less than the supply, and English exports went into a tailspin, dragging the economy down with them. England suffered a severe depression until its exchange rate was finally reduced to about $4.

An undervalued exchange rate also brings problems. Now there is an incentive for foreigners to buy cheap exports or assets of the undervalued country. Foreign money will flow into its banks, raising the money supply. As the money supply increases, inflationary pressures also increase. The country will suffer from rising prices.

Thus we can present the problem of exchange rates that are too high or too low in this fashion:

Overvalued (too high) exchange rates lead to unemployment.
Undervalued (too low) exchange rates lead to inflation.

Defending the dollar, then, means finding an exchange rate that will roughly balance our total supplies and demands for foreign exchange for transaction purposes and capital flows. When the dollar falls, it means that we have not yet found such a rate. The verdict of the marketplace, at least until quite recently, is that the dollar is too high. We know this is the verdict because the demand for dollars vis-à-vis marks and francs and other strong currency has been steadily less than its supplies.

What happens when the dollar falls? Clearly we move from the dangers of an overvalued currency toward those of an undervalued one. That is, a falling dollar spurs our exports and helps employment. It also makes imports more expensive. Alas, in our inflation-prone economy, this results not just in fewer imports, but in another fillip to the price level. Oil prices go up because of the falling exchange rate, along with the price of Hondas and TV sets, coffee and tea.

The net effect of a falling dollar is therefore measured, in part, by the benefit we ascribe to expanding employment minus the cost we assign to higher inflation. As we have seen so often, most people place a higher priority on inflation than on unemployment. We welcome the boost to exports but put more emphasis on the boost to the cost of living.

Unfortunately, that is not an end to the problems caused by a falling dollar. For in addition to its real costs and benefits, a falling dollar imposes a large—although diffuse—threat. In the end it is this threat, perhaps even more than the actual effect on employment or prices, that makes the problem of defending the dollar so difficult.

The threat is that the falling dollar will induce a serious crisis in the world economy. Foreigners who hold American assets calculate that their wealth has diminished because each dollar is worth less in their own currencies. To many people, especially in business and finance, the news of a falling dollar conveys ominous implications about the state of the U.S. economy. Bankers worry lest international depositors switch funds from U.S. banks to foreign banks, straining the liquidity of the American financial system. Americans who own stocks and bonds worry that the dollar is weak, and begin to sell. A falling stock market and a slumping dollar can cause some corporations to rein in their capital expenditures. These actions in themselves may be sufficient to bring about a genuine financial panic and a fall in GNP.

There is still another repercussion. The government watches these developments with distress and seeks to prevent such a panic. It tries to defend the dollar in various ways, including raising interest rates to attract foreign funds and cutting spending to show its determination to stop inflation. And so the fear of a crisis induces government policy that will bring on a recession. A falling dollar can thereby lead to a falling economy.

What Can Be Done?

Can we prevent the dollar from falling? Of course we can. Do we want to? That depends on the politics of the question—on who gains and who loses.

One way of defending the dollar is simplicity itself: Prevent the flow of imports from rising. Anything that will turn the balance of merchandise payments in our favor will unquestionably alter the supply-demand situation and strengthen the dollar.

Is this a sound policy? It will hardly come as a surprise when we say that the answer is a political, not just an economic judgment. To be sure, there are certain kinds of imports that we would like to diminish not merely to defend the dollar, but to strengthen the nation. For instance, if we can substitute domestic energy (such as solar or coal) for imported oil, or if we can cut down on oil imports by conservation methods, the United States will gain a much-needed measure of strategic independence as well as helping the dollar.

If, however, we cut down imports by blocking cheap shoes, textiles, or steel from abroad, we are simply protecting inefficient industries at home, and penalizing American households and businesses by depriving them of the right to buy shoes, textiles, or steel as cheaply as they otherwise might. We can sharpen the point by imagining that our tariff wall was sky-high. Then no goods would come into the United States. Would that be good for America?

On the other hand, imports cost jobs. Even if we compensate the workers in threatened industries, or help relocate them, or retrain them, some will not make the transition and will remain unemployed. There is a real human cost to competition—from abroad or home—that should not be lost sight of. Should we let one hundred thousand steel or auto workers go down the drain just to get cheaper steel or autos?

Most economists would say that in the end, the benefits to the economy of having cheaper foreign goods, plus the benefits of moving our own resources and labor away from inefficient uses, outweigh the costs of unemployment. It would be interesting to see if they came to the same conclusion if we were to import cheaper economists from abroad, asking our domestic practitioners to find another way of making a living. But even if we accept the conventional wisdom, we can see that there is a real conflict of interest involved in defending the dollar through restricting imports. That is, of course, the political nub of the matter, and it is this political issue—Who is to gain? Who is to lose?—that must be satisfactorily resolved before we can really address ourselves to the economics of the question.

What about helping our exports? Many countries have tried to help their exports by giving subsidies of various kinds to their producers, so that they could sell their wares abroad cheaply. We have subsidized some exports by underwriting our merchant marine, by arranging for special deals on U.S. arms sales to foreign nations, and by foreign-aid policies that have permitted us to sell large amounts of farm products abroad.

As with imports, it is not possible to give black and white answers about the wisdom of defending the dollar by export assistance. It may be in the national interest to sell eight billion dollars of arms on easy terms, or to export one billion dollars of foodstuffs to the underdeveloped nations under Public Law 480, but these policies should be judged on their own merits. The fact that they help defend the dollar is not, and should not be, a controlling consideration.

Policies to help exports or to hinder imports affect the balance of payments on current account. But there is also the market for foreign exchange for capital purposes. Can we defend the dollar by intervening in that market?

We recall that there are two basic kinds of transactions in the capital market: direct investment (purchasing plant, equipment, and other assets abroad), and portfolio investment (buying stocks and bonds). We can, of course, defend the dollar by simply passing a law preventing United States companies from acquiring foreign assets. The difficulties here are twofold. The first is that any interference with the free movement of capital tends to lower the efficiency of the market system. We have been reluctant to abridge the right of corporations to invest their funds wherever they can yield the highest return, whether at home or abroad.

In addition, the stream of profits from our overseas investments constitutes one of the strongest supports for the dollar. In 1979, for example, there was a demand for sixty-six billion dollars as the earnings of our foreign-located plants were sent back to the U.S. Against that flow was thirty-four billion dollars leaving the country as the earnings of foreign companies sent to their various home nations. In this international flow of repatriated earnings, the U.S. is clearly a big gainer. Any restriction on the outflow of direct investment will sooner or later diminish this source of dollar earnings.

A second way of defending the dollar in the capital markets is to seek to attract portfolio investment or short-run capital into the United States. This can be done by raising interest rates to bid for the pool of funds that shops in the world's money markets.

We have already seen the problem with this method of defending the dollar. Raising interest rates in order to increase the flow of money into the United States exerts the same effect on the economy as raising interest rates for any other reason. Investment is discouraged. Spending slackens. The economy slows down. The price of defending the dollar is therefore to expose the economy to further unemployment.

THE DOLLAR AND INFLATION

We begin to see that there is a connection after all between the falling dollar on the international exchange and the falling dollar in terms of purchasing power. Policies to defend the dollar abroad are closely linked to policies to defend it at home. That is, the measures needed to bring about a stable supply-demand situation with respect to the international value of the dollar are closely related to measures needed to bring about a stable supply-demand for dollars and goods at home. Fighting the fall in the dollar is therefore much like fighting inflation, with all its familiar difficulties. If we clamped down on all growth in the United States, for example, and allowed a really large rise in unemployment, we would stop or greatly slow down inflation and simultaneously rescue the dollar. The recession at home would cut deeply into imports, and that would redress the balance on current account. The fall in profits of American firms would discourage U.S. investment abroad. And a sharp rise in   interest rates to fight inflation would tempt foreign speculative and short-term funds into American banks and bonds.

All this, however, comes with a very substantial price tag. We have seen that political realities make it very difficult to consider an all-out recession as a cure for inflation. Even more surely, the American public would not tolerate a deep depression as a cure for the falling dollar, an ailment that mystifies most people. Instead, the cry would likely go up for stiff import quotas or for restrictions on the foreign investments of American companies—policies that also impose costs on our economy, but not such visible costs as a recession.

There is still another way of arresting the fall of the

dollar. It is to use the resources of our Federal Reserve System to support the dollar.

All central banks in all nations, including the Federal Reserve, operate in the foreign exchange markets, supporting or depressing the price of their currency against foreign currencies. They can do this because they all hold supplies of foreign currencies—yen, marks, francs, dollars, and pounds, as well as gold certificates and other international assets. Thus when the Fed defends the dollar, it does so by entering the exchange market as if it were a Swiss, a German, or a Frenchman. It simply offers the currencies of these nations, asking dollars in return. In using their buying and selling powers, the central banks are not permitting the price of their currencies to be set just by the forces of supply and demand, but by "dirty floating"—free-market price plus or minus the demand of the central banks.

This means that the ability of the Federal Reserve—or any other central bank—to intervene in the market is limited by the supplies of foreign currencies or gold or other international assets it has on hand. Take gold. In 1980, U.S. gold reserves totaled about 260 million ounces, worth (at over $600 per ounce) about $160 billion. The Federal Reserve could, if the government so directed, use all of that gold to support the dollar. If it did, undoubtedly the price of the dollar would rise substantially, but would it stay at its new higher price when the gold had been used up? Not unless the basic forces of supply and demand had been permanently affected by the rescue operation—a doubtful assumption.

Curiously enough, a government is always able to lower the price of its currency because it can easily sell unlimited quantities of its own money on the foreign-exchange market. But its power to buy its own currency is inherently limited. It can step in to stem a speculative rout, but it is unlikely that it can much affect a falling price trend that emerges from the current and capital flows of the world.

THE VIEW FROM ABROAD

Actually it is not only Americans who are eager to stop the dollar from falling; foreigners are also eager to have stable exchange rates. Consider how the situation looks to them as the dollar weakens. The price of American-made goods keeps steadily declining. Conversely, the price of their own goods becomes ever more expensive in America. Thus, just as there is an outcry in America against the falling dollar, so there is an outcry abroad. Therefore, just as the Federal Reserve may step in to defend the dollar by selling its supplies of foreign currency, foreign banks may also find it in their interest to defend the dollar by selling their own currencies and buying dollars. Much time at international financial conferences is devoted to efforts to work out a coordinated defense of the dollar (and sometimes other currencies) by the joint action of several key central banks. What is always the bone of contention at such conferences is the proper exchange relation. Countries that depend on exports want their currency to be cheap in the world markets; countries that depend on imports want their own money to be dear so that it will buy a larger amount of other currencies.

We can see that defending a currency is not only a difficult policy to devise, but a difficult policy to define. But we have left out of consideration a matter of much importance for the United States. It is that the dollar is not merely the currency of this country; the dollar has become a world currency. It is the currency in which many central banks hold much of their own international reserves. Japan, for example, holds billions of U.S. dollars as part of its foreign-exchange wealth, along with gold and other major currencies. In addition, there are at least five hundred billion U.S. dollars (some estimates run much higher) in European bank deposits. These foreign-located dollars, some owned by European individuals and companies, some by American, are called Eurodollars. They are one of the means by which the world carries on its vast international business.

The presence of these enormous quantities of dollars held as the reserves of other countries, or as the monetary medium of the world, adds further importance to the need for a stable dollar. When the dollar falls, it imperils the international value of foreign reserves and foreign deposits, and there is always the risk that central banks or corporations will rush to dump their dollars before a further fall occurs. Once again we have the danger of a self-fulfilling speculative disaster. So the dollar has to be defended to secure international economic stability even more urgently than to secure purely American interest.

NEW INTERNATIONAL CURRENCIES

How can the dollar be defended against a worldwide assault— or simply against worldwide nervousness? One possible way is for the dollar to be replaced by other monetary units as the world's reserve currency. To some extent this is slowly happening as other strong currencies, such as German marks and Swiss francs, are gaining the place formerly occupied by U.S. dollars. Alongside the five hundred billion American Eurodollars, there are perhaps as much as one hundred billion dollars worth of Euromarks, and there are other smaller international reserves denominated in Swiss francs, in yen, and in other currencies.

A second means of taking the strain off the dollar is the rise in the price of gold. In 1980 the supply of gold in the official reserves of various nations was down slightly in physical quantity from 1971—from 1 billion ounces to 931 million ounces. (The difference, plus the gold production of the intervening years, was now owned by private individuals). But the value of the 931 million ounces, with gold selling at over

$600 an ounce, was far larger than formerly. The value of the world's official gold reserves in 1980 had soared to almost $600 billion. This gold was worth more than half the value of the total reserves of all the world's central banks. Without ever having decided to do so, say the champions of gold, the world is returning to a gold standard. If it does, the role of the dollar will be much less critical.

No one can foretell what will happen to the future price of gold. Therefore let us consider one final way of relieving the dollar of its international burden. This is the gradual adoption of a wholly new money standard invented by the International Monetary Fund (IMF), a part of the World Bank set up under the auspices of the United Nations. This new monetary unit is called an SDR, special drawing right. It is a kind of "paper gold"—an internationally recognized currency available only to central banks, and linked by the authorities to gold and to other main currencies.

SDRs are now held by all the major countries of the world in addition to gold and to supplies of each other's currencies. But SDRs have the special advantage of being issued under international control. There is no way that the world can deliberately bring about an increase in the quantity or value of gold. There is no way that the world can change the value or the amounts of dollars or marks or francs available as international reserves. But the nations of the world can agree to augment the value of SDRs, and by using these to settle international payments in place of dollars, they can gradually relieve the dollar of the task of being the world's principal currency, with all the risks attached thereto.

To sum up, we can see that defending the dollar means many things. It means finding a place for the American economy that will roughly balance its flows of payments to and from the rest of the world. It means, once again, finding a resolution between the fears and panics generated by inflation and unemployment. It means finding a compromise between the interests of consumers in inexpensive foreign goods and the interests of particular groups whose livelihoods are threatened by competition from abroad. (To be sure, lives can be disrupted by competition from an industry located right next door, but the strains are magnified a thousandfold when the competing industry is located far away and manned by workers and managers of another culture, another color.)

There are no simple solutions to these economic and political challenges. Indeed, the prevailing bias of nationalism causes us to read threats into situations that are, in fact, achievements. Americans generally regard it as something of a failure on their part that the West Germans have surpassed our standard of living and that the Japanese are rapidly approaching it. We still hanker for the past when it seemed an immutable (and therefore entirely proper) fact of economic life that American living standards would be two or three times higher than those of the next wealthiest nations. The thought rarely strikes us that it is not a failure but an immense success that a rough parity of material well-being has finally been achieved among nations that share a common heritage and that hold many political goals in common.

The attitude of competitive vying among nations is an ancient scourge, one that has led innumerable times to war. It is very unlikely that defending the dollar "against" our Western trading partners will lead to war in our time. But the threat of antagonism and friction now arises from a hitherto ignored quarter, the underdeveloped regions of the world. For a new attitude is evident in the nations of the East and South that are exposed to the full blast of the technology, organization, and ideology of Western capitalism. The supine acquiescence that enabled the West to have its uncontested way with the underdeveloped world is giving way to an attitude of resistance—still uncoordinated and largely ineffective resistance, but resistance nonetheless. The rise of OPEC, to be discussed in our next chapter, is one manifestation of this change in attitude. Whether or not OPEC will be followed by other cartel-like arrangements that would radically change the economic balance between the capitalist West and the underdeveloped rest is still uncertain. What *is* certain is that the stance of independence and defiance symbolized by OPEC will become a permanent element in international economic life in the future.

Thus, defending the dollar will pose new difficulties in the coming decades. More than ever the challenge will revolve around political factors, namely finding some viable balance between the interests of Americans (or of the West as a whole) in maintaining their privileged position in the world, and their interest in a stable world order. It would be foolish to predict the outcome of this impending contest, but we must expect these economic and political pressures to impinge on our lives for a long time to come.

FIVE

LIVING WITH
LESS ENERGY

It is a commonplace that we are living through an energy crisis—a crisis that becomes visible every time there is a sudden gas shortage, and lines of cars with fuming drivers besiege the harried owners of neighborhood gas stations. Less well understood is the fact that we face more than a crisis. Together with all other industrial nations, we are living through a transition period in which we are being forced to change our energy-using habits, to look for new energy sources, to redesign our energy-generating and energy-consuming technologies. On the success with which we handle this transition will hinge a great deal of our collective well-being. If we handle it poorly, we could be severely penalized by a substantial fall in our living standards. If we handle it intelligently, the fall will be less severe, perhaps hardly noticeable at all. Many of the choices before us hinge on engineering and scientific considerations about which economists have nothing to say. But there are important aspects of the future that depend directly on economic decisions and economic reasoning; these are the aspects of the era of transition to which we will address ourselves first. And in the background, as always, politics ...

THE GAS SHORTAGE OF 1979

The energy problem, as we shall soon see, goes far beyond oil. Nevertheless, a good place to start unraveling the problem is the gas shortage of 1979. Suddenly—more or less out of the blue—there wasn't enough gasoline to go around. Drivers filled their cars on alternate days of the week, sometimes waiting for hours as long lines inched to the pumps. Violence flared up; cars were burned; a few persons were actually killed. What lay behind that mysterious shortage?

The basic reason was simple enough. A revolution in Iran had severely disrupted oil production in that country, which was then supplying ten percent of the world's exports.

Five million barrels of oil per day were cut off from the world's supply. As a consequence, within a few months a relationship of supply to demand that had been in slight surplus turned into shortage. There was simply not enough crude oil to allow the refineries to keep retailers' tanks full.

Then why didn't the price of gas shoot up to whatever prices supply and demand indicated? The answer is that the government regulated the price of gasoline and would not allow the market to clear. Why not? Because the administration and Congress were both fearful of the political outcry that would have attended three-dollar or four-dollar gas. A shortage with all its hang-ups, seemed preferable to rationing by price.

To analyze the immediate supply-and-demand situation of 1979 is, however, to view only the tip of the iceberg. For the question that comes immediately to mind is why the United States, for many years the world's largest oil producer, was so dependent on foreign oil? The question turns our attention away from the crisis of 1979 to the historic trends leading up to that dramatic year.

Actually, the United States had been dependent on oil imports for a long time before 1979. Already in 1960 we were importing a fifth of our domestic consumption. By 1970 imports had grown to a quarter of national use. And by 1979, when the gas shortage occurred, the fraction had risen to almost fifty percent.

The reason for the increase was simple. Shortly after World War II the oil fields of the Middle East, especially in Saudi Arabia, became the object of intensive exploration and development. Soon it became evident that the Middle East contained vast reservoirs of oil, dwarfing American fields in size, and far cheaper in cost. A study in 1960 declared that the average cost of production in the Middle East was $0.16 per barrel, compared with $1.73 in the United States.

Therefore the growing availability of Middle Eastern oil posed a serious competitive threat to U.S. oil producers. As a result of their lobbying efforts, import quotas were introduced in 1957, limiting the amount of foreign oil that could be brought into the country. This protectionist policy was justified—as nearly all protectionist measures are—in the name of national security. Ironically, the best way to have protected our nation against a possible emergency would have been to import as *much* foreign oil as possible, conserving our own supplies against a future crisis. Had we done so, we would not today be quite so critically dependent on foreign supplies.

Our quota policy assured a market for U.S. producers, as well as stupendous profits for the major oil companies who bought oil at Middle East prices and sold it at U.S. prices. Meanwhile, however, the volume of United States consumption was growing by leaps and bounds. In 1960 total domestic consumption of oil—domestic plus imported—was still under ten million barrels a day. But each year consumption increased as the American automobile fleet expanded and as oil displaced coal as a prime source of energy for utilities. In 1960 coal provided two thirds of the fuel used by utilities. Within ten years it was barely more than half. Oil and natural gas made up the difference. By 1979 domestic consumption had almost reached the twenty-million-barrels-of-oil-per-day level.

While demand for oil was dramatically growing, domestic supplies of oil showed an alarming tendency toward leveling off. Already by 1950 the curve of new oil discoveries had begun to turn down like a curve of diminishing returns. As geophysicist Owen Phillips has written:

> The first billion feet of drilling in the United States yielded discoveries of ninety-five billion barrels of oil; the next, twenty-four billion; the next only seventeen billion, a dramatic indication of the diminishing return as the search for new oil becomes ... increasingly expensive.*

---

*Owen Phillips, *The Last Chance Energy Book* (Baltimore: Johns Hopkins Press, 1979), p. 43.

Today there is no dissent from the conclusion that the discovery curve has peaked, bringing with it an inevitable peaking in production. Even the confirmation of the vast Alaskan oil fields in 1970 was no more than a spike on a trend that was decisively headed downward after 1950, as the next chart shows.

The gas shortage therefore pointed to a profound problem for the United States. Our energy requirements were much greater than we could possible fill with our domestic resources. By the end of the 1970s our domestic energy requirements for all purposes came to the equivalent of about forty million barrels of oil per day. As the table shows, oil and natural gas supply about three quarters of our energy, with other sources supplying the rest.

Rate of U.S. Oil Discovery

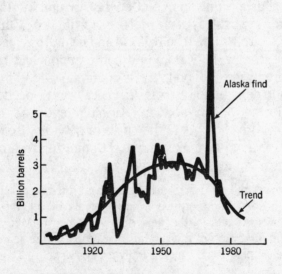

Source: Owen Phillips, *The Last Chance Energy Book* (Baltimore: Johns Hopkins Press, 1979), p. 39.

Energy Sources, 1977

	Percent
Petroleum	45
domestic	*23*
imported	*22*
Natural Gas	28
Coal	19
Nuclear	4
Hydro	4

The extent of our dependency on foreign energy is now clear. Let us put that dependency into focus by taking a quick overview of the main uses to which we put our total energy.

Energy Uses, 1978

	Percent
Transportation	26
Residential and Commercial Heating	38
Industrial Power	32
Petrochemical	4

In round numbers, we can see that by the end of the 1970s we were dependent on imported petroleum for almost the equivalent of the energy that powered our entire transportation fleet of cars, trucks, planes, and trains. Alternatively, we can think of our dependency as equal to sixty percent of all the energy we used to heat our homes, office buildings, stores, and factories. Or we can think of it as providing the energy for three quarters of all the power generated in our utilities and factories.

The 1979 gasoline shortage was therefore only the tip of a very large iceberg. The American economy has become crucially dependent on imports of foreign oil to maintain its normal operation. Any substantial cutoff of oil would virtually bring the system to a halt.

THE WORLDWIDE OIL SQUEEZE

The United States is by no means the only nation in an oil squeeze. Indeed, because we still produce half of our own oil, and not least because we are the fortunate possessors of enormous coalfields, we are relatively fortunate in the world-wide energy situation. Sweden and Japan, for example, depend almost one hundred percent on imported oil. Germany and France are far more dependent than we.

And the dimensions of the problem take even larger shape when we widen our lens from our own squeeze to the supply-and-demand situation of the entire planet. Then we see that the energy crisis is even broader and deeper than at first appears. Indeed, the crisis is best thought of as the beginning of an era of energy transition—away from oil to coal, perhaps nuclear, and then solar sources; and even more important, away from the careless use of energy to an era of careful economizing of our most important single input.

How much oil is there in the world? We do not know the answer to this with the certainty that enables us to make reasonably firm projections of American supply. For example, new discoveries of oil in Saudi Arabia have exceeded oil production in that country every year, so that reserves in that vast oil area are still rising. Then, too, the recent discovery of the Mexican fields, perhaps rivaling those of Saudi Arabia, indicate that important new reservoirs of oil undoubtedly still exist.

The problem is that until very recently world oil demand has been growing faster than supply. For example, between 1960 and 1978 the world automobile fleet tripled, from ninety-eight million vehicles to over three hundred million. By the end of the 1970s the world's automobiles alone consumed one fifth of all the oil produced in the world. And world demand for oil for electric-power production, heating, and petrochemical use has also grown apace, along with Western GNPs.

The result is that the situation we saw in the United States is beginning to be reproduced on a world scale. The vast Mexican find is, like the Alaskan find, only a spike on a trend of worldwide oil discovery that now seems to be leveling off or heading downward. By the end of the 1970s, despite the Saudi fields, worldwide proven reserves (including United States reserves) were for the first time shrinking. As a special analyst in *Business Week* put it: "The beginning of the end of the oil age is now in sight."

The cheap oil of the late 1950s and 1960s lasted until the Arab-Israeli War of 1973. During those years the Organization of Petroleum Exporting Countries (OPEC) was formed to bargain with the oil companies about oil prices and the sharing of oil revenues between the companies and the producing countries. At first very weak, the bargaining position of OPEC was gradually strengthened by the steadily mounting demands for oil. But the balance of power did not really shift until the 1973 war. Rallying its members against Israel and her Western supporters, OPEC was able to impose an embargo on shipments of oil to the West. Within a year oil prices had gone through the roof, from three dollars to about twelve dollars per barrel.

This was perhaps the boldest, and certainly the most lucrative, exercise of oligopolistic market power ever seen. Within a year the OPEC nations were receiving a flow of $112 billion a year from the world, a flow sufficiently large to worry many Western observers about its effect on worldwide solvency. (The Arab countries avoided that danger by recycling their petrodollars to the West through imports from and investments in Western nations.)

Despite cries of outrage from the West, the OPEC price managers were, in all likelihood, only acting as profit maximizers. OPEC oil prices were not the highest possible prices, but prices that were calculated to maximize revenues after taking into account the effect of those prices on consumption, on the search for substitutes, and (in the case of so strategic a commodity as oil) on political or even military repercussions. As a result, from 1974 to 1979 the price of oil was largely unchanged; in fact, in terms of an inflating world price level, oil actually fell in real terms. Then in 1978 the Iranian shah was overthrown and oil production in Iran abruptly declined. Other nations, notably Saudi Arabia, increased their production somewhat, but the world market suddenly became tight. The price for spot oil—oil sold for immediate delivery rather than on a long-term contract—jumped by as much as eight dollars above the basic contract price of thirteen dollars a barrel. Some emergency deals were made at prices up to thirty-five dollars per barrel.

The enormous rise in oil prices has encouraged the development of a new view among OPEC producers. Originally eager for a rapid inflow of funds for purposes of economic development or luxury consumption, some big OPEC producers—especially in the Persian Gulf—today find themselves awash with foreign exchange. They cannot spend their existing revenues without creating further inflation. All of them have therefore lengthened the period over which they plan to exploit their oil. Their rational course of action, in the light of expected higher oil prices, is to cut back on oil production. This will not only hold down the unwanted inflow of foreign exchange, but will also prolong the life of their physical reserves.

There is no way in which worldwide supply-and-demand curves for oil can be reliably projected into the future. But all indications point in one direction: Prices are very likely to increase. The reasons are these:

1. As we have just seen, some Middle East OPEC producers are likely to cut back on oil production to avoid an unwanted inflow of unspendable foreign exchange.

2. Political instabilities similar to those that have resulted in the Iraq-Iran War may arise elsewhere in the Arab world. Any political change in Saudi Arabia or Kuwait or the other feudal oil sheikdoms is likely to result in curtailments of deliveries to the West.

3. World oil demand is still rising. After the crisis of 1973, Western nations have economized considerably on oil. The rate of growth for petroleum products has diminished from seven percent a year to two percent. Nonetheless, the demand for oil is still growing, and this too serves as a force for higher prices.

These considerations have led virtually every observer to conclude that the probable trend of world oil prices will be up, perhaps very sharply. Last year the CIA and other informed agencies predicted that oil would reach a price of over fifty dollars a barrel (in today's prices) by 1995. That already seems low. Even optimistic observers now expect that oil prices will rise by at least fifty percent within the next few years.* Almost certainly we will have to adjust to further oil shocks in the future—and indeed, until we have completed a transition to a less oil-dependent world.

How will the prospective rise in oil prices affect the American economy? One way will be to encourage the development of alternative energy supplies. As the price of oil increases, sources of energy that were formerly ignored because they were too expensive become attractive for investors. We see this in schematic fashion in the chart that follows.

In the late 1950s the demand for energy was sufficient to render profitable the exploitation of U.S. oil and gas, hydroelectric power, and our more easily accessible coal. (As we know, had it not been for the quota system, oil prices in the

---

*Robert Stobaugh and Daniel Yergin, *Energy Future* (New York: Random House, 1979), p. 39.

United States would have been much lower and we might well have relied almost completely on oil imports.) Today, the higher price of petroleum has made coal in general and even high-cost nuclear energy competitive with oil. Ahead lies the development of synthetic fuels and solar energy, all of which are today still too expensive for commercial use.

THE ENERGY SPECTRUM

It takes a very sophisticated knowledge of engineering to evaluate all the possibilities for expanding and redirecting U.S. energy supplies. But the principal avenues are clear enough:

Conventional Oil and Gas

According to the latest U.S. Geological Survey (1975), it is highly probable that U.S. reserves of crude oil amount to 220

The Energy Spectrum

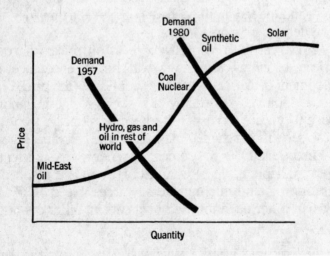

billion barrels. This is enough to supply our consumption for about 20 years at existing rates of use.

Of course, new reserves will be found. But they will be more expensive and smaller in extent, and will not be enough to arrest the steady shrinkage in our total oil reservoir. This puts into perspective such finds as the much-heralded discovery by Houston Oil and Minerals of thirty to forty million barrels of oil in a Texas county that was supposedly bone dry, having been picked over and drilled since the 1930s; Houston's discovery is enough to satisfy U.S. consumption for about two days.

There have been about two million wells drilled in the United States, so we can be fairly secure that no vast undiscovered resources remain—with one exception. Perhaps as much as two-thirds of the oil in an oil field remains underground, despite drilling, because we lack the means of bringing it to the surface. Higher oil prices will encourage the use of expensive techniques such as injecting steam or chemicals to dissolve that oil. It is hoped that as much as fifty percent of these residues may be directly salvageable by using mining techniques.

Shale

Just beyond oil lies oil shale, a form of petroleum-laden rock that has long tantalized energy producers. It is estimated that the Green River formation of Wyoming, Utah, and California contains as much as a trillion barrels of oil locked into its shale.

The problem again is one of cost. The present or prospective methods of extracting or burning shale are still too expensive to justify commercial use at today's prices. In addition, the processing of shale on a scale adequate to supply a substantial portion of national needs would involve enormous indirect costs; a whole landscape would be chewed up, and vast quantities of water (in an already water-short region) required to put the process into operation. Thus shale is still a distant prospect. "A production level equal to about a half of 1 percent of U.S. oil consumption—100,000 barrels a day— would require a billion dollars and a decade for development," write Robert Stobaugh and Daniel Yergin in the much-acclaimed Harvard Business School report on *Energy Future*.

Coal

By everyone's agreement, coal is the energy source nearest at hand, at least in the short run. In all likelihood, coal production will rise by fifty percent or more during the next decade. Unlike the case with oil, we have ample supplies from which to draw these expanded outputs. There is enough coal in the United States to last for three hundred years, even if we expanded coal output by five hundred percent.

But coal has problems. It is a fuel that lends itself poorly or not at all to the biggest demand for energy—the tank of the automobile. Coal is a highly polluting energy source, requiring vast investments in scrubbers and other equipment to prevent utilities or homeowners from inflicting costly damage on the landscape and the people in it. Coal production will almost certainly be expanded by using strip mining, and the social cost of this environmental damage is also very large. Not least, coal has traditionally been a backward industry—low in research, poor in labor-management relations and safety. During the last decade, sixty-five hundred lives were lost in coal mining.

Many of these problems can be corrected if coal now becomes the recipient of massive doses of technology and capital; but experts do not see coal as a panacea. The general expectation is that coal output may rise by about fifty percent during the next decade. That will pose enough difficulty in terms of environmental impact and will require the development of new technologies for mining, transporting, and using coal. It will bring some relief to our energy problem, but it will not solve it, at least not within the threatened period ahead.

Nuclear Power

Ten years ago nuclear power seemed the solution to all energy problems. Today it is regarded as one of the biggest and most intractable of the energy problems.

The reasons for the turnabout are three. The first has to do with the growing public awareness of, and anxiety about, the safety of nuclear plants. The accident at Three Mile Island in 1979, the gradual news of a possible major nuclear accident in the Soviet Union in the early 1970s, and the continuing debate among scientists over the problems of storing radioactive wastes have all generated public alarm and have considerably altered the attitude of the government itself. There is today a general feeling of "wait and see" toward the development of nuclear power along the lines of today's technology. As a consequence, each year since 1970 the projections of expected nuclear capacity have been reduced, and a virtual moratorium is now imposed on the industry.

Second, there is a growing awareness that today's technology, even were its problems entirely resolved, is only a short-term solution. This is because the existing technology "burns" uranium—and uranium itself, like oil, is in restricted supply. Here again diminishing return has taken its toll. Geophysicist Phillips writes: "In 1956 the discovery rate in terms of pounds of uranium oxide per foot drilled was 18.6; in 1968, when exploration was much more intense, it had dropped to 6.9, and by 1973 it was only 2.4." According to modern resource estimating techniques, by 1975 we had already extracted thirty percent of all the recoverable uranium in the nation.

Third, new technologies that could vastly increase the extent of nuclear power are either dangerous or undeveloped. One of these techniques is the breeder method of creating power, which actually creates more fuel than it uses. The difficulty here is that the fissionable substance is not uranium but plutonium—the metal that is the basis of atomic weaponry. Any large-scale shift to breeder technology would enormously magnify the danger that atomic explosives would fall into the hands of small nations or even terrorist groups. In addition, breeder technology is still in its infancy, and no large-scale shift to breeder plants is even imaginable short of several decades from now. In the distant future beckons the possibility of developing fusion power, a limitless source of energy. But fusion power is still a laboratory experiment, and scientists are by no means convinced that it can ever be obtained for more than the millifractions of a second during which fusion power has been generated in a few labs.

These uncertainties make it impossible to predict the long-term role that nuclear power will play. Possibly it will one day be entirely safe and in abundant supply; but there is no possibility whatsoever that nuclear power can play more than a marginal role during the period of energy transition immediately before us. Over the next decade or two, nuclear power will remain a long-term hope, not a short-term actuality.

Solar

Solar energy presents an attractive long-term alternative source of energy. When we speak of solar energy today, we mean utilizing the energy of the sun directly or through very short-term intermediate processes, as when crops grown by solar input are then used as fuel (biomass). Direct uses of solar energy include using atmospheric heat or sunlight to warm (or cool) buildings, focusing sunlight on a massive power tower, using the atmospheric turbulence created by the sun's heat (wind power) or the temperature differentials of sea water (ocean thermal processes), or converting sunlight directly into electricity (photovoltaic cells).

As we would expect, all these uses involve difficulties of one kind or another. Solar home heating is a promising source of energy for certain areas of the country, but has no application to transportation. Wind machines are noisy and irregular. Biomass requires the use of land areas whose growing potential may be required for foodstuffs. Ocean thermal processes require mile-long tunnel-sized tubes suspended in the ocean. Power towers necessitate means of storing power for use when the sun is not shining. Photovoltaics are still in their infancy.

These difficulties in no way detract from the promise of solar power, but they indicate that we cannot expect to move directly into a solar era. Estimates of the proportion of our total energy that could be supplied by solar techniques by the year 2000 vary widely. Long-term projections, involving a radical reshaping of our energy inputs and uses, envisage a very large-scale reliance on solar energy—but only after fifty years of massive technological change. Estimates over a shorter range, up to the year 2000, vary from seven to twenty-three percent of total energy—with, however, the contribution steadily rising. It is certainly possible that late twenty-first century America will be a solar economy, especially if large R and D is soon begun toward that end. But there is no chance that late twentieth-century America can look to the sun to replace its dependence on oil.

Conservation

There remains one source of energy that we have not discussed—a source that requires no exotic technology, that is safe and clean and immediately at hand. It is conservation. Another way of describing it is to call it efficiency, for conservation means not just using less energy (after all, if our oil supply were to be cut off, we would perforce "conserve" oil), but using energy much more effectively.

We have already begun to utilize this hitherto neglected source of energy. The rise in energy prices has brought about relatively simple energy-saving responses, but this is only the beginning of a potentially much larger energy input. The cumulative fuel savings from bringing American automobiles up to federally established standards by 1985 will be equivalent up to the year 2000, to the output of two Alaskan north slopes. That is tantamount to making two such fields (twenty billion barrels) available for other uses. By avoiding waste and by using industrial heat to produce local energy (cogeneration techniques), the consumption of industrial energy can be reduced by twenty-five to forty percent. Home insulation has been estimated to reduce fuel needs by up to sixty-seven percent. In all, calculations show that for 1973 the standard of living could have been obtained with forty percent less energy input. This is the equivalent of all the oil—not just the imported oil—used that year.

To be sure, the savings of conservation are once-over changes, not constantly regenerating changes. A more efficient automobile engine reduces our fuel use per mile in the year it is introduced, but does not drop it further each successive year. If conservation is to provide a continuing source of energy, we must improve our energy efficiency each year, getting ever more productivity from each ton of coal or barrel of oil. It is likely that diminishing returns will be encountered here as elsewhere, so that we can look to conservation for dramatic short-term savings, but not for continuing long-term energy support.

ENERGY INDEPENDENCE

Can we then achieve energy independence without a serious fall in our living standards? It must be clear that the challenge is a formidable one; it is nothing less than converting an economy designed to operate on two-dollars-per-barrel oil to one using forty- or fifty-dollars-per-barrel oil. Can we, in short order, change the location of our homes, the design of our transportation systems, the configuration of power networks and industrial plants to reflect the altered requirements of a world where the cost of energy has increased by two thousand percent?

The answer is that we cannot gain this kind of energy independence quickly. For the rest of this century, at the very least, we will have to cope with the problems of running an industrial economy that is no longer economical in terms of its energy inputs. If we are faced with drastic cutoffs of oil imports, this may mean making painful adjustments in our economic processes—radical cutbacks in driving, heating, lighting, and perhaps even in producing. If we are fortunate and enjoy only moderate cutbacks in imports, we can work toward a balanced energy supply for the late 1980s, as shown in the table below.

Sources of Energy
(millions of barrels/day, oil equivalent)

	1977 Actual	Late 1980s Potential
Domestic		
Oil	10	10
Natural Gas	9	9
Coal	7	11
Nuclear	1	2
Solar and Hydro	1	4
Imports		
Oil	9	9
Gas	0	1
Conservation	—	8
Total	37	54

Source: Stobaugh and Yergin, op. cit., p. 232.

In this scenario, conservation and solar energy provide two thirds of the growth in energy supplies, and imported oil does not rise at all. *This still leaves us vulnerable to an oil cutoff.* We would not have achieved energy independence in the sense of national self-sufficiency. But we would be on the way toward achieving as much independence as can be hoped for in the short run. Furthermore, we would be pointed in the right direction for achieving an appropriate energy structure for the long run.

So much for the economics. Now the politics. Who has gained, who has lost, in this enormous shift in the energy situation? The winners are relatively easy to identify. The rise in world oil prices has resulted in a tremendous increase in the value of United States oil reserves. After the 1973 oil hike alone, U.S. oil reserves were worth eight hundred billion dollars more! Their value will rise with every hike in world oil prices. Assuming that existing and improved techniques will allow us to extract two hundred billion barrels of oil, a rise in oil prices from twenty-five to fifty dollars will create instant oil wealth worth twenty five dollars times two hundred billion, or over five *trillion* dollars.

Who will share in this bonanza? The immediate winners, if oil prices rise to world levels, will be the owners of U.S. reserves—mainly the big oil companies and, of course, their stockholders. These companies are among the largest in the U.S. economy. In the famed *Fortune* list of five hundred industrial companies, five of the top ten are oil companies.

Although oil has always been a favored industry in the United States, the government has been unwilling to allow it to reap the huge rents that would accrue from selling domestic oil at world prices. Instead, the government has regulated the price of oil sold in the United States, allowing domestic oil to rise much less than would be the case in a wholly unregulated market, and establishing a series of different prices for "new" oil, "old" oil, and many levels in between. The result has been a maze of regulations that have resulted in some reduction in profits to the oil industry. The transfer of wealth from consumers to producers has been checked but not entirely avoided, and profits of the oil companies have risen substantially. The profits of American oil companies were $8.5 billion in 1970 and $29.5 billion in 1978. A windfall-profits tax, passed in 1979, should garner $9 billion per year by 1981.

Other winners will be those industries whose products will be favored by the energy shift. Coal mining should become more profitable. Any company that develops a successful solar energy device is sure to gain. And employees and stockholders connected with winning industries will also be benefited by the energy shift.

These are the winners. Who are the losers? Consumers are losers, of course. But not all consumers are equal losers. Much depends on two considerations: where you live and in what income bracket you find yourself.

Take regions first. The Northeast is twice as dependent, per capita, on heating oil than the West. The Southwest is almost a third more dependent on gasoline than the Northeast. A family living in a Florida city spends much less on heating or driving than a family that lives on a Montana farmstead.

Second, income brackets. Energy in its various forms, from heat to gasoline, plays a larger part in the budgets of poor families than well-to-do families. This is because energy is largely used for essentials. For families in the lowest ten percent of households, energy accounts for a full third of household expenditures; whereas for households in the top ten percent, it absorbs only five percent of household expenses. Therefore, a jump in energy costs will penalize the poor much more severely than the rich.

We have spoken of the consequences of higher energy costs in terms of our capacity to carry on business as usual, or with reference to our well-being as consumers of gasoline or heating fuel, or as employees of favored industries. But there is also a general cost imposed on us all by virtue of the diffusion of higher costs throughout the entire economic structure.

About ten percent of our cost of GNP derives from energy. Thus, to the extent that energy prices rise substantially, they may by themselves constitute one of the driving forces of inflation. That is a worrisome prospect for the short-term future. If world oil prices rise fifty percent in the next few years, as some observers expect, that would in itself impose a five percent hike in the price level. If oil prices double, our domestic prices will go up ten percent on the average. There is no way of avoiding that inflationary blow altogether. We can only seek to limit its impact by choosing the short-term, high-gain energy path of conservation, while we work as hard as possible toward the long-term route of nonpetroleum energy inputs.

ENERGY POLICY

How shall we run our economy to achieve as much energy independence as possible—including independence from oil-induced inflation?

By and large we can distinguish between two kinds of action that must be taken to assure our relatively safe passage through the decades ahead. The first has already been alluded to many times in our discussion of the energy spectrum. It is the need to encourage massive new energy sources, from shale and coal through solar.

Much of this initial investment will have to be made by the government, directly or through subsidy, along the lines of its successful attack on nuclear energy in the 1940s and on space travel in the 1970s. Indeed, the development of the atom bomb and of the series of satellites and space vehicles suggests the scope and extent of the effort that must be made.

The reason this phase of our energy policy must be carried out under government auspices is that the size of the needed research effort, the riskiness of the various alternatives, and the long-time span before commercial success is likely, all make it impossible for private enterprise to mount an all-out attack. Certainly private R and D (research and development) will supplement public R and D, but the main thrust of the campaign to bring forth a new technological base must of necessity be placed under government responsibility.

Yet despite massive effort, a switch to new energy sources cannot take place overnight, as we have seen. For the next decade or two we will have to rely heavily on the one source of energy that is instantly available—conservation. And here the choice between market or planning is more complex.

If we are faced with a sudden cutoff of imported oil, as might be the case if revolutions continue to disturb the Middle East, it would surely be necessary to resort to warlike measures of allocation—including the rationing of scarce supplies of gasoline and heating oil—in the interests of national security and order. But short of such an emergency, there is reason to think twice about the hasty use of government regulation.

The most efficient rationing mechanism for goods in short supply is still the market. Allowing gasoline and oil to reach their true market values (or using sales taxes to raise them to world market levels) is the only way to indicate the actual opportunity cost that reality has imposed on us. When we allow gasoline, for example, to be sold for less than its true cost, we encourage individuals to consume it as if it were easier to obtain than is the case. Inevitably, that excess consumption creates problems such as long queues at gas stations. We then have to intervene with nonprice conservation measures, such as 55 mph speed limits or regulations about thermostat settings. These regulations may be justified on their own merits of safety or health, but they are not to be recommended as ways of reducing consumption.

In the end we will no doubt rely on both market and regulation to achieve conservation. If gasoline becomes very expensive, our democratic ethic will likely incline us to treat it as a kind of public good, of which each person is entitled to a fair share. If gasoline remains affordable, we will probably allow price to play the main allocating role.

These considerations should make it plain that many of the choices forced upon us by the need to shift our patterns of energy production and consumption plunge us into political dilemmas. Can we find ways of persuading Montanans, for example, to allow their landscape to be defaced in order that easterners may have enough coal to heat their homes? Or to air-condition their homes? Can we persuade those who oppose nuclear power that a certain level of risk is worthwhile to maintain a steady flow of electricity to light our cities? Or to run our dishwashers? Can we educate a nation accustomed to consuming energy as if it were almost a free good to give up its snowmobiles, its powerboats, its energy-consuming packaging, its two cars in every garage?

As before, these questions involve profoundly difficult problems of political leadership and compromise, as well as economic calculations of plus and minus.

A SPACESHIP ECONOMY

One last problem should be faced. The energy squeeze can be mitigated, as we have seen. Our standard of living can be maintained, at least for a while. But no one any longer takes for granted that we can continue to race into the future on the path of self-feeding growth that propelled us in the past. At its roots, the energy situation arises from the barriers that all such systems must sooner or later face: Either they will outpace the ability of their resources to sustain their growth, or they will bump into barriers of pollution or ecological danger generated by their mushrooming growth.

The energy squeeze is the first serious brush that our expanding industrial system has encountered with these constraints of nature. Even if enormous new energy sources are discovered, it is unlikely that our growth trajectory could be sustained more than another generation or two. Our industrial processes are already threatening the environment in other ways than that of energy exhaustion. Perhaps the most serious threat is the greenhouse effect that results from the continuously growing addition of carbon dioxide to the atmosphere as a by-product of energy use. Carbon dioxide in the air acts like window glass in a greenhouse, trapping the air that has been heated by the sun. Scientists expect that dangerous consequences could follow from another fifty years of unrestricted increase in combustion. The National Academy of Sciences has warned that we must throttle back on combustion if we are not to disturb the earth's climate. Roger Revelle, chairman of the Academy Panel on Energy and Climate, has said, "We will have to kick the fossil habit by 2050."

What is certain, then, is that all industrial systems, socialist as well as capitalist, will have to change their attitudes toward growth in the coming decades. In the words of economist Kenneth Boulding, we will have to give up the idea of our society as a "cowboy economy" and embrace that of a "spaceship economy"—one in which outputs are not just thrown away, but used as parts of a great process of "throughput" by which mankind recycles its wealth to disturb as little as possible the delicate ecological system on which it depends.

This perspective begins to make us aware of the complexity of the problem of energy and growth. Basically, energy is needed to bring growth to a world that is, in most nations, still desperately poor. Yet growth is already beginning to threaten a world that is running out of environment. Ahead lies the formidable problem of a world in which growth may encounter ecological barriers on a worldwide scale, bringing the need for new political and economic arrangements for which we have no precedent. The Age of Spaceship Earth is still some distance in the future, but for the first time the passengers on the craft are aware of their spaceship's limitations.

And this, too, is a political problem. At bottom it represents the need to compromise the demands of two constituencies, one of which is articulate and powerful, the other of which is mute and powerless. One constituency is ourselves, living in the present and asking that our immediate needs and wants be filled by the energy sources that still exist in abundance. The other constituency does not exist at all, for it consists of men and women not yet born, of the posterity whose standard of living—indeed, whose life itself—will depend on the decisions that we make today.

What are the claims the future can exert on the present? What should we do for posterity? What has posterity ever done for us? On these political questions ultimately hinge the decisions we will make regarding the challenge of living with less energy. Political, you will ask? Are these not moral questions? Precisely. But all political questions are ultimately moral ones. The only difference is the degree to which political decisions stir our conscience. And it is, of course, our conscience—and only our conscience—that must be the spokesman and advocate of the generations to come.

A LAST WORD

There you have the five challenges: coping with inflation, overcoming recession and unemployment, facing up to the realities of taxing and government spending, finding our place in the world economy, adjusting our way of life to the energy sources available to us.

What should we do in the face of these challenges? Our first answer is very simple: *Understand them*. By understanding them, as we have said so many times, we mean not only learning the facts and interconnections that constitute the economic aspect of these challenges, but also becoming aware of the clash of interests that is their hidden political core. Laying bare this core is essential because it is the part of the challenges that is usually ignored. In the name of conservatism, we are offered endless programs for a return to the free market, to the gold standard, to a lower level of government involvement. What is usually missing from these programs is a presentation of their political costs and benefits—a discussion of who will gain and who lose; of which regions, industries, groups, and income brackets will win, and which will not.

Our second answer is more complex. There are many economic proposals that *might* help us deal with the challenges. Whether in fact they *will* help depends almost entirely on the political consensus we have achieved. Take, for instance, the problem of inflation. The most effective way to deal with inflation, all economists agree, is mutually to curb our incomes and our spending, perhaps through taxation, so that we all become inflation fighters, and no one bears an undue portion of the cost. But of course that takes a degree of political will and unanimity that today seems impossible. Lacking that general will, the best answer may be some kind of wage and price controls that, in effect, force some of us to become inflation fighters, while the rest of us go about our business as before. But even that takes a political willingness on the part of the great unions to volunteer for a thankless job. Lacking that, the best we can do may be little more than the clumsy and

largely ineffective off-again, on-again monetary and fiscal restraints we have lived with for the last several years.

The same analysis holds for the challenge of overcoming recession and unemployment. If we have achieved the
political accord that permits us to take strong anti-inflation
measures, we can obviously move much more vigorously to
expand the economy than if no such accord exists. So, too, we
can adopt much bolder employment-generating programs if
there has been a change of mind with respect to the appropriate role of government. Lacking such a change, we must
accommodate ourselves to the reach compatible with our
present suspicious and grudging attitudes. But to achieve such
a change of mind is also a political requirement, a political act.

Even a goal as seemingly bland and universally ap-
proved as lifting our productivity depends on our political
capacities. For example, the ability to shift resources from
failing regions and industries into promising ones depends on
our political determinations, for those resources include
voting, perhaps protesting, men and women. In the same way,
our ability to defend the dollar or to shape a long-run energy
program also hinges on the compromises and agreements we
can impose and accept, the political resistances we can
effectively meet.

In a word, it is politics that sets the limits for economics.
So we will not give a list of the "best" proposals for dealing
with the five challenges. There is no such list. There is only
what we can do, given our moral values, our political attitudes.

Because these values are all-important, we should lay
our own on the table:

> We favor a politics of economics that spreads burdens and
> sacrifices as widely as possible, rather than imposing them on
> particular groups, especially weak and defenseless groups.

> We favor a politics of economics that takes into account the
> severity of the damage that may be inflicted on individuals in

the name of the public good, and that is generous in compensating them for that damage.

We favor a politics of economics that places the gains from a fairer income distribution high on the national agenda, perhaps even higher than economic growth with worsening income distribution.

We favor a politics of economics that looks on the costs and benefits of government economic activity with the same impartial calculation that it applies to private economic activity—and vice versa.

Finally, we favor a politics of economics that accords to the aims of justice and decency at least equal consideration to those of efficiency and market freedom.

We announce these values not to proselytize for them—it is too late for that—but so that our readers cannot accuse us of having failed to disclose our political leanings. But in any event, our aim is not to make converts. As our readers must by now be weary of hearing, it is to set forth the challenges as clearly and as honestly as we can, so that they can come to their own determinations, however different from ours.

Whatever those determinations, the great question remains—whether democracies can make thoughtful, reasoned choices, beset as they are with special pleading, distracted by commercial enticements, encouraged to seize the day and to forget the morrow. That critical question can only be answered from experience. We will have to find out what an informed public can achieve. The first thing, however, is to inform it, to pose the task itself. In a small way, that is what *Five Economic Challenges* has tried to do.

INDEX

135